The Arresting Tales
of Michael F.

By Michael F. Bohan

Foreword

I am a man who likes to talk. More specifically, I like to tell a story and believe you me, I have had plenty of material in my eighty eight years on this earth to give life to a yarn or two. The forty-two years which I spent in An Garda Siochana yielded a wealth of experiences, from the comrades I worked with, the characters I met and the criminals who crossed my path. Some were amusing, some were tragic, but most of all they were experiences that were special and made their mark on me, so much so, that years afterwards, I can still recall them in minute detail.

On more than one occasion, family and friends have been entertained by my tales and told me that I should commit my stories to the written page. Growing almost weary of hearing, 'Ah Michael, there's a book there', I did begin to put some words on paper. I found that I enjoyed writing and when I retired from the job in 1987 I managed to put some stories together which received a favourable response from anyone with whom I shared them. Encouraged by this, I began to think about doing it on a more formal basis. However due to the deteriorating eyesight, not to mention an uncooperative tremor in my right hand, it began to be quite a challenge. Then I found someone who was willing to visit me at my house and transcribe the stories I had carried around in my head for all those years.

The result is here within these covers. To put it all into context, we've gone right back to the beginning, to my lovely native County Leitrim. It's a tale of times and ways long past, the likes of which, as they say, we will never see again. I hope you will find as much pleasure in reading my story as I have had in recalling and re-living it. I have changed the names of some of the characters, specifically in those stories where the protagonist may not have been depicted in a particularly favourable light, but apart from this, please know that everything here is completely founded in truth, unbelievable though some of the tales may be! I hope you enjoy them all.

***

I come from the small town-land of Cloone, in County Leitrim, which was home to just five families when I was child. We lived in a single storey thatched house, with two bedrooms and one kitchen/living area. I was the middle son of three, Sean was born on 22 June 1922 and Peter was born on 15 September 1929. I will give you my own date of birth now though I will have to explain that I have three different dates to choose from.

According to my parents I was born on 18 March 1925. In 1944 I filled out an application form for An Garda Síochána, putting down the birth date my parents gave me. I was then asked by Head Quarters, (HQ), to submit a birth certificate and sent off for one from the Registrar of Births and Marriages in Carrick-on-Shannon. When I received, it I was extremely bewildered by the fact that I appeared to have been born on 28 May 1925. Naturally I applied to my mother for an explanation; 'I thought I was born in March?'

'And so you were', she replied. I wasn't convinced, 'But look at this birth cert!'

Now, my mother was a pretty astute woman. She nodded agreeably, 'Yes, I see it has you born and registered on exactly the same day, which would almost never happen. Babies are usually registered weeks or even months after their birth date. You were born in March but the Registrar – God bless him – was an alcoholic and must have mixed up the dates, hence the mistake.'

That accounts for two of my birthdays, with certificates to prove it.

Following my beloved wife Nancy's death from cancer in 2002, I applied for a Widower's Pension, which I think might now be called a Survivor's Pension. For some reason I had to send in my Baptismal Certificate so I wrote to the parish priest in Cloone, asking him for the certificate and supplying a donation for his efforts. He duly sent me the cert along with a letter in which he wrote, 'Sorry to disappoint you Michael, but in fact you are a day older than you thought you were, according to your Baptismal

Cert that is. You were actually born on 17 March 1925!' Unfortunately my mother was no longer around to check with; in other words, at this point, I remain confused as to which date is the right one.

My father, John Bohan, was a road ganger; that is, he worked on repairing the roads. Later on he became an over-seer, supervising a number of gangers himself. In 1937 a local government grant of £40 was made available to anyone wishing to extend their dwelling house. My father applied for it and added two bedrooms, a sitting room and utility room. The thatch was removed and replaced with the ultimately more modern slates.

My mother, Brigid Kate née Murray, was from Drumdoney, in the parish of Aughavas, just outside Cloone. An attractive woman, she always maintained that she was the nicest looking girl in her parish and naturally none of us ever challenged that statement. She was also a skilful house-keeper and a wonderful cook with the plainest of ingredients. Her speciality was the traditional Leitrim dish of boxty. There are three kinds of boxty: boiled, pan and loaf, and all are made primarily from potatoes. Boiled boxty consisted of potatoes that had been grated and drained, with flour and salt added to them. Mother made them into dumplings and sat them into a saucepan of boiling water. The water had to be kept on a constant boil otherwise they sank ungracefully and glued themselves firmly to the bottom of the pan. Whenever my brothers and I were going out for the day Mother always made sure we took boxty with us, she reheated it on a pan with slices of home-cured bacon. It made for a nourishing and delicious snack. In fact it was all that we had unless we sold the cattle or pigs. There just wasn't the money for fancier food. Pan boxty was nice too, a simpler dish whereby the potatoes were cooked like pancakes with salt and flour. However, the "Daddy" of boxty was surely the loaf because in addition to the potatoes, salt and flour, were currants, raisins and candied peel. Once a famous dish in Leitrim and Mayo, I am sad to note its decline today.

Our house was a popular one in that most evenings we had visitors in to play cards or else listen to my mother read aloud from the *Irish Independent*. Some of the neighbours couldn't read but were eager to know what was going on in the world. Mother was a willing hostess and always made sure there was plenty of tea in the pot. During the war, when tea was rationed, she even bought black market tea which was illegally retailing at one pound and ten shillings; a proud woman, she would never have anyone say that Mrs Bohan didn't give them a cup of tea and usually a bite to eat as well.

I am somewhat hazy regarding the exact details of how my mother and father met but this is the story that was passed onto me. When my mother was about seventeen years of age she had her first glance of my father as he drove home in a horse and cart, and found him quite handsome indeed. They eventually met properly and "walked out" together, as it was called back then. Her parents would not consent to a wedding because they felt my mother was too young so the young couple hatched a plan. Although I wonder if her parents' reluctance had something to do with the fact that she only had one sister and one brother and both of them had immigrated to America when she was a child. They may have hoped that she would stay at home, so that she would be there to look after them in their old age, which was often the case with children who never married or left the family home. In any case the couple were committed to a future together and were not about to allow anyone else to interfere with their plans.

My father went over to Newcastle, in England, where he got a job on the docks with his brother. He saved his wages for a few weeks before sending for my mother. They were married over there on Easter Monday 1919, by an Irish priest in a Catholic church and remained there for the next three years until my eldest brother, Sean, was born on 22 June 1922. He was a sickly baby and the doctor advised my mother to bring him back to Ireland where my father got a job working on maintaining the roads around Leitrim.

There were a lot of Bohans in the parish of Cloone, so in order to differentiate between them; it was a common enough practice to be given a nick name. Accordingly, my father, who was six foot four inches tall, was known as Tiny Bohan. His brother Michael, a large, well-built figure, famous for his strength, was nick-named "The Tiger". He once lifted a 600lb garden roller one foot off the ground in a bet for a pint. My Uncle Francie was known as "Smudger", I don't know why. Uncle Charlie was "The Plasterer", which of course would have led most people to believe that such was his occupation. Except of course, it wasn't! There were plenty of other distant Bohans, cousins of my father, who were also liberally sprinkled with odd names, the reasons behind them long forgotten: Packie the Spider; Paddy the German; Little Paddy; Joe's Paddy and Thomas' Paddy. Fortunately for them, women were spared this particular indignity.

We were very fortunate in Cloone in that we had a lot of bog land at our disposal, from which we made our own turf from the mud we raised at the bog. Making the turf was serious business, requiring help from the neighbours, and me being kept home from school. My job was to drive the donkeys through the mud to break it up. We would go round and around in endless circles within the plot, the eldest of the five donkeys on the inside where there was less walking to do. Buckets of water drenched the mud beneath the donkeys' feet. When the mud on the surface was well and truly broken up, I would drive the donkeys out of the plot to allow the mud to be turned upside down.

At this stage the neighbours arrived, the men in their bare feet with their trouser legs rolled up and shovels at the ready. When they finished I drove the donkeys back onto the plot again, more buckets of water were flung over the freshly turned mud and we retraced our steps in the same circle.

The mud was tested by putting our hands in it. If it came up without any lumps it was ready for running. Two men started at the top left corner of the plot and used their hands to divide the mud into rectangles of 8 inches by 4 inches. By the time they finished you could barely see the imprints of their fingers in the soft bricks.

It was Nature's turn next. Depending on weather conditions the turf was left to dry for up to ten days before it could be lifted. Each sod would be lifted individually and set on end. Ten days later, the turf was dry enough to be stood in rows, two by two, in layers, where it was left for three weeks until it could be put into clamps, or stacks. Three weeks after that it could be brought home and stored in the shed. There was always surplus turf which my father would sell in July, finally receiving the money in the last week of November, "Hollantide", as was the custom back then. This was to do with the practice of taking grazing rights over a field. You removed your animals from the field in the last week of November to give the land a chance to rest for a month. It was simply good farming practice. My father rented our surplus bog land to people up the road and that rent money would be paid by Christmas. Thanks to the bog we always had plenty of money, which meant a good Christmas, not that my parents would have regarded us as being well off but we never knew the want of a shilling.

Every year my father would buy a pig, fatten him up and have him killed in November. The man who did the killing and butchering was Pat Doyle. He never took money for his efforts; all he wanted in exchange was a couple of day's labour from my father on his own land. My mother stuffed the stomach with a mixture of oatmeal and herbs amongst other ingredients, to make black and white pudding, while slices of bacon hung from our ceiling to be cured by the kitchen fire. As you might imagine, the smell was wonderful.

About a week before Christmas my parents would take a cart to the village to purchase the Christmas foodstuff. The markets were set up for the evening, allowing the husbands to finish their day's work. A typical yuletide sight was the line of carts, belonging to our friends and neighbours, snaking their way into the village on a winter's evening. There was a bit of snobbery attached to this event. It was regarded as shameful if you were spotted grocery shopping in the first week of the New Year because it meant that the family hadn't enough money in December to tide them over. It was a case of tuppence half-penny looking down on tuppence!

Father Peter Conferey was our popular parish priest who had started out as the curate in Drumlish, County Longford. An extremely pious man, he once walked, in his bare feet, the 140 mile trip from Drumlish to Lough Derg. It was his own penance for himself. When he first came to Cloone, he was on crutches, having broken his right leg. It was said that at some stage he was in danger of losing his sight so he prayed to God to send him any affliction other than blindness. He retained his sight and, after getting rid of

5

the crutches, got himself a walking stick which accompanied him everywhere.

I served mass for him for six years. A deeply religious man, he a was priest before his time and a great organiser who did a tremendous amount of work for the community. Apart from saying mass and hearing confessions, he visited the sick and also each of the five local schools at least once a week. Every Christmas he gave a party for the children where every single child got a present. He went to Dublin every December to buy four hundred presents which he then wrapped himself. To qualify for a present we had to bring something we made to the party. One Christmas, when I was nine years old, I made a wooden stool and was duly rewarded with my Christmas present from the good priest.

Perhaps I owe my love of reading to this man. He set up a tiny library that consisted solely of paperback westerns by the likes of Zane Grey and Louis d'Amour. This was my first ambition, to be a cowboy who ate beans at the ranch after a long day in the saddle. I daydreamed about using that saddle as my pillow and sleeping with a rifle lying across my chest. Years later when I had my first taste of baked beans, I discovered I had no taste for them, so perhaps it was no bad thing that my cowboy dreams never came to fruition!

Father Confrey was only fifty-seven years old when he died suddenly on Saturday morning, 18 April 1938, after suffering a heart-attack. When a priest dies his will must be read before he is buried. On hearing of Father Confrey's passing, Frank Pope, the local undertaker rushed off a telegram to Dublin, ordering an expensive solid, mahogany casket. In the meantime the will had been read in which Father Confrey asked to be buried in a homemade coffin. So, the local carpenter made a coffin for thirty shillings and poor Frank was left with his expensive purchase. However, God works in mysterious ways. Another priest, Father Blessing, a native of Cloone, who had spent his ministerial life in New York, had recently returned home for his retirement. He died about three weeks after Father Confrey and was buried in the mahogany casket.

***

Today some members of the travelling community may have a bit of a dubious reputation but I only have the fondest of memories of a travelling family that came to live in Cloone. Mr McCauley, a well-known tinsmith, and his wife had seven or eight children, and lived between two small caravans until the parish built a timber hut for the family in which they settled permanently. The children went to school in Cloone and the family came to the mass every Sunday. Mrs McCauley called to our house every Saturday evening and my mother would always bring her in and give her tea, bread and butter and sometimes a plate of rashers and sausages. Mother would also give her a bag of flour, when she was leaving, so that she could bake her own bread.

One summer's evening, my twelve-year old brother Sean and I were out playing in the fields. All the children went barefoot in summer time. In fact there was always a bit of competition to see who would be the first to brave the elements and turn up for school in their bare feet. The only boy who didn't take part was the shoe-maker's son. Poor Sean stood on a broken bottle, opening up his heel. The blood was everywhere and Mother was doing her best to stem the flow when Mrs McCauley arrived. As soon as she saw the blood she turned and ran down to the hayshed, coming back a few minutes later with a handful of cobwebs that she spread over Sean's foot. Miraculously, it stopped the bleeding almost immediately. I have heard it said that there is some derivative of penicillin in cobwebs, which may explain their healing properties, but how true that is I don't know.

***

Sergeant Tommy McDermott was the local Garda. Married to a local teacher, he was a decent man. He applied the law in a practical and sensible way; there was no splitting of hairs for him. I would imagine that he wasn't the busiest of sergeants since Cloone was, for the most part, a law-abiding community. Obviously there must have been the occasional misdemeanour and summary offences such as unlicensed dogs or people cycling after sunset without a light on their bikes.

He also had to visit the schools to check up on any absenteeism. It was obligatory for national schools back then to submit in a weekly report of which children had been absent and the Gardaí were bound to investigate each case. If the same child was marked absent on two further occasions, the parent or guardian was prosecuted under the School Attendance Act 1926, which stated that every child, aged between four and fourteen years, was obliged to attend school, as long as the school was available to the child, within four miles of his or her home. Regarding a first offence the probation act was applied. A second offence was met with a fine while the third offence meant that the child was deemed to be a 'perpetual offender' and sent off to an industrial or reform school until they turned sixteen years of age. Remember now that it was rarely the fault of the child that they were absent, the parent or guardian were usually to blame, with farm labour being the most common excuse, yet it was the poor child that got sent to one of these awful places for a crime they did not commit. Recent history has shown how some of those unfortunates were treated.

I am grateful to this day, that throughout my subsequent career in An Garda Siochana, that I was never involved in a case that resulted in any child being sent to such a place. It would have been a dreadful weight on my conscience.

**

We had six local shops in Cloone; one was run by Maggie Mitchell who was a kind and charitable person. Next door to her was Maggie Garvey's huckster shop; she sold cigarettes amongst other things. In those days Woodbine cigarettes came in paper packets of five, costing two pence each. When Peter, my brother, was seven years old he took himself off to Maggie Garvey's for fags. At that time you could buy five Woodbines for tuppence but Maggie would sell two Woodbines for a penny to children, giving her an extra profit.

Someone must have fooled her once with a bad coin as she developed a ritual of checking money handed over to her. There was a flag stone in the centre of the shop, she would take the coin and come out from behind her counter to bounce it off the floor. If it made the right tinkling sound it was real and she was sufficiently satisfied to complete the transaction.

Peter handed over his penny which was proved to be genuine and arrived home with his two Woodbines. He sat himself down in front of the fire and lit up. He had taken just one pull of his fag before he was caught by my mother who shrieked, 'How dare you! You little brat, smoking at your age!' Perhaps it might have been better if she had gone and shrieked at Mrs Garvey for selling them to him in the first place!

There were four primary schools in Cloone and confirmations were held once every three years with much preparation involved. For four Sunday evenings prior to the Confirmation Day, classes of girls and boys were brought to the church for an examination in Catechism and the Bible by the priest. Each child was asked four questions every Sunday and if they so much as stumbled in their answer they were sent back to a lower seat.

One evening Charlie Kilkenny, a very intelligent boy, was asked his sixteenth question, 'What is forbidden by the fifth commandment?' Poor Charlie immediately started listing out what was commanded by the fifth commandment. However, he realised his mistake and stopped himself to answer the question correctly. It was no use. 'Back! Back!' said the priest and Charlie could only walk to a seat at the back of the church, his cheeks glowing with shame.

The children who answered all sixteen questions correctly, over those four days, wore their achievement on the day itself, with a white ticket that was either pinned to the lapel of their suit, if it was boy, or the top of her dress, if it was girl; in other words it was clearly visible to everyone in the church what level they had achieved in their examination. Those who missed one or two questions had to wear a blue ticket. The children who missed a lot of their questions didn't wear any ticket at all and they were known as the "dunces".

A few weeks beforehand my mother washed two sacks and put them hanging in the hay shed to dry, warning Sean and me that if we did not get a white ticket we would be wearing the sacks for our Confirmation Day. Fully convinced of the sincerity of her threat, we diligently applied ourselves to our religious studies in the intervening weeks.

Sean and I were duly confirmed, with white tickets, on Sunday, 10 May

1935 by Bishop McNamee, along with seven "dunces", four boys and three girls.

To this day the practice of separating children with coloured tickets, and categorising some of them as dunces astounds and annoys me. Can you imagine the psychological damage to the children who missed questions, to have their ignorance highlighted in front of their families and everybody else? One of those so-called dunces that I was confirmed with ended up in Birmingham, working on a building site. He eventually became a major building contractor himself and a millionaire to boot.

***

One important feature in the daily lives of the people of Cloone, as indeed in all of rural Ireland in those days, was the 'cures'. Back then, poor people did not have the benefit of social welfare payments. If the doctor was needed, a member of the family would have to go and petition an elected member of the local county council who had the authority to issue the applicant with a red ticket. The ticket, which represented five shillings, the price of a doctor's visit, would be given in lieu of money. At the end of the month the doctor would submit all his tickets to the local authority and would receive the corresponding payment. Naturally it was regarded as a slur on the family if a red ticket was required to pay the doctor.

However, there was an alternative to the doctor, especially in rural areas like Cloone. We were lucky enough to be able to avail of some of the local "healers". One summer both Peter and I came down with the mumps, our throats were sore and our necks were swollen. We were in a bad way.

Now, by tradition, the only days for making cures were Mondays and Thursdays. I never knew why. In any case my mother sent Peter and me over to our neighbour Pat Mitchell, a farmer, who had the cure for mumps. There was a lane, approximately 300 metres in length, leading up to his house. He took each of us in turn, put his donkey's blinkers and reins on us and, removing his cap, drove us three times around the pig sty while saying prayers. When I think about it now there is something almost pagan about the whole thing, although as children this wouldn't have occurred to us, so we were always willing and compliant participants. However, seeing is believing! When he finished, Peter and I left to walk home. By the time we reached the road at the other end of the lane, we were both free of pain and swelling.

Willie Casey, another neighbour of ours, performed the cure for worms. You don't hear so much about this condition nowadays but when I was a child it was a common ailment. They were small, white worms passed with a bowel movement. I was about seven when I got them.

It was a Monday morning when my father brought me to see Willie. First of all he had to diagnose that I did indeed have them. For this he had a simple procedure. He used a green ribbon, about one metre long, and two white threads of the same length. He placed one thread front and back of the ribbon and then put them under my shirt, next to my heart. Leaving my father and me he went off into the next room for a few minutes. I believe he spent the time there saying whatever the relevant prayers were. On his return he removed the ribbon. The two threads were now on the same side of the ribbon which confirmed that I definitely had worms and, therefore, needed the cure. He went outside and took some moss, rubbed it under my nose and – hey presto! – The worms were gone. I'm a believer, I was there!

No money was ever exchanged for these treatments. The most these men ever wanted was a day's work from my father on their farms. Other local healers included Mrs Mullanney who cured jaundice with a concoction of boiled briar leaves that had to be taken three times a day. Peter Gannon cured a bad heart over three visits in which he prayed over you. There is no logical explanation as to how or why such cures appeared to work and to the modern mind they likely seem primitive and as I say, almost paganistic. Maybe it was a combination of the homeopathic properties of some of the herbs and plants used along with the power of prayer and belief. All I truly know is that they did cure people as I was a witness to this on numerous occasions.

***

When I was twelve years old, and my brother was fourteen, we both decided that we would like to own a dog, and not just any dog, but a greyhound who would hunt wild hare for us. My mother was immediately opposed to our choice of breed, explaining that 'Greyhounds are not affectionate!' Typically my father rallied in support of our petition being the soft man that he was. 'Ah, Bridget, let them have their dog'.

Permission granted, we promptly made an appointment to visit the Durnan family, having heard that Mr Durnan had a greyhound that was in need of a good home.

On Friday evening I took some twine with me and set off on the two mile walk to the Durnan residence. They were a large family and lived in poverty. When I arrived at the front door it swung open to reveal the entire family huddled around an ailing turf fire. On the outside, doing his best to find a way closer to the flames in vain was my new pet, Dawn.

Mr Durnan told me the dog was a pure thoroughbred and that he had the papers to prove this, papers I never got to see for myself. On meeting Dawn my Uncle Francis laughed, 'The only paper that dog has ever been near is the *Leitrim Observer*!' adding, 'You might need to tie some wire to his tail to help him turn'. It was true that the dog had a very short tail indeed for a greyhound but I would not be deterred by this minor anatomical deficiency. In my mind, Dawn was going to be a champion!

In the end my uncle was proved right when Dawn proved himself to be thoroughly useless. The following Sunday we took him out in search of hare, boasting to my mother of all the dinners we would provide. We met up with some friends who both owned a 'proper' greyhound and went hunting together. As we walked along, a hare jumped up from some feet away from us and sprinted off across the field. The other two dogs shot off but Dawn lagged far behind appearing anything but interested in his quarry. Although, to be fair to him, he had been standing a good distance away from where the hare had been hiding. So we had no blame to attach to him.

A few days later and perhaps due to his hunting exertions, Dawn fell ill, developing pneumonia. There being no question of veterinary intervention, Sean visited the chemist in Mohill to enquire about the best way to treat him. He was told to put a plaster of mustard around his chest and ribs and, above all, keep him warm. The two of us diligently applied the mustard plaster and left the patient sleeping in the hay in the shed. Meanwhile, Mother, seeing our concern for the poor dog, had an old seal skin coat, which had been a present from her own mother. She carefully laid it over Dawn who seemed to appreciate the warmth of his cosy cover. Another week passed before Dawn felt strong enough to leave the shed and cross the road to our house. The sight of him in the fancy coat, the sleeves of which were dragging along the road, was a memorable one for the neighbours who were coming out of evening mass. Thereafter, Dawn had the accolade of being the best dressed dog in the parish!

A week later, Sean and I took Dawn out for a second trial. This time, as we walked along the ditch, a hare shot away from just beneath our feet, with acres of flat land to cross at breakneck speed if he were to save his skin. This he managed easily enough, since Dawn's reaction was rather less than satisfactory for a predator. My lasting impression of this scene was a hare fleeing in charged terror with a surprisingly unconcerned dog in casual – if not downright accidental – pursuit. Sean felt betrayed, 'That dog's worse than useless. We'd catch more hare on our own.'

Poor Dawn didn't have much time to prove himself after that. As it turned out he was to die a couple of weeks later from natural causes. There was no inquest.

***

The Missions were a popular bonus for mass-goers when I was growing up. Our church hosted plenty of visits from priests who had spent time spreading the Word of God throughout foreign lands we had never heard of. One time we were privileged to have two Redemptorists from Limerick to give the mission. The church was packed with stalls set up outside to sell religious medals and souvenirs.

Big Pee Kilkenny lived three miles outside Cloone. Once a month, he made the journey to Cloone to collect his old-age pension before making his way to Brady's Pub where he would drink as much as he could afford. His son would arrive to collect him in the evening with the pony and trap. The pub was run by Dolly Brady, a very religious woman who, during the course of a mission would close her pub early, at a quarter to seven so that she could attend the mission mass. Big Pee was quite drunk by this stage but nonetheless decided that he would go along too. He sat half-way up the church and promptly fell into a drunken sleep, his neighbours doing their best to ignore the snores.

Meanwhile the mass had started, the highlight of which was, by some appropriate coincidence, a dramatic sermon on the evils of intoxicating liquor. The priest promised life in Hell for all eternity for those who fell under its spell, condemning it loudly as a "Mortal Sin". He pressed his point home by asking, 'And how long is Eternity?' It was a rhetorical question and thus he was ready to answer it himself, 'Well, let me tell you! Imagine a robin arriving once a year to take a sip out of the Atlantic Ocean. By the time that robin has completely drained the ocean your time in Hell would not even be half over.' Sticking fast to this point he described how there were two clocks at either end of Hell, 'On the first clock the two hands are pointed at "Never" and on the second clock the hands are pointed at "Forever"!' He paused to let this sink in amongst the congregation who, rather than focusing on strange clocks and damnation, found themselves in wonder at the volume of Big Pee's snores. Charlie Curran was sitting beside him and elbowed him in the ribs, causing Big Pee to wake up and call out, 'Dolly, fill me up another pint there while I fill me pipe!'

Big Pee was married to Mags whose sister kept house in Chicago for a wealthy Jewish family. She must have been on great money since she was able to send presents back to Ireland three times a year as would have been the tradition among families where a son or daughter had emigrated. One summer she sent clothes to her sister and brother-in-law. That Sunday Big Pee turned up at mass wearing what he and Mags believed to be a casual 'summer suit' that was appropriate for Chicago's warm weather. The Kilkennys lived in isolation and, as a result, were fiercely ignorant of trends and fashions. For instance they had never heard of a suit of pyjamas and if they had, they would never have imagined that men might wear them. So, there was Big Pee dressed head to foot in luminous green silk pyjamas, with one of Mags's belts around the gaping neck line, pulling it together, and the dainty trouser legs tucked into his wellington boots! The story of Big Pee's summer suit generated much talk for months to come around the village. As a result, any subsequent 'parcels from America' were carefully examined, the contents identified and their purpose accurately established before they were certified as being suitable for parading at mass.

***

I was, in general, a happy scholar from I started attending the local primary school at the age of four years and a few months. That said, on my first day, our teacher, the kindly Mrs Cooney, was taking the lesson outside as it was a fine day and on spotting my father passing by on his horse and cart, I decided that I would join him on whatever outing he was embarking on. When Mrs Cooney had her back turned, off I ran calling after my father until he slowed down sufficiently for me to manage to climb on board. He explained to me that my place was in school and in any case Mrs Cooney who had by now noticed my absence had arrived in hot pursuit. I was duly 'persuaded' to return to join my fellow scholars and thus began my first of some ten years of education.

Mrs Cooney taught the infants and first and second classes. Third, fourth, fifth, sixth, seventh and eighth classes were instructed by Master Tom Moran, a strict disciplinarian but a brilliant teacher. He somehow managed to teach all six classes in the one room which was no mean feat when you consider that he was trying to instruct his pupils in everything from the basics of reading, writing and spelling for the younger children to the more advanced subjects of algebra, Latin and Shakespearean plays for the more senior students.

I was a good pupil who applied myself diligently to my studies, although we all tried our best as Master Moran was not a man for entertaining any slacking or insurrection in his classroom ! Many was the unfortunate student who incurred his wrath for a missed spelling or an incorrect line in a poetic recitation and returned home from school that day with smarting hands as a result of their erroneous ways. His methods would not be condoned today but they worked at the time and I can tell you that all of us benefited greatly from the education we received.

Schooling for most ended when they reached eighth class usually around the age of fourteen having completed the Primary Certification. There was no means of advancing to study for the Leaving Certificate as there was no secondary school in the parish of Cloone, the nearest one being located in Carrick-on-Shannon which was run by the Marist Brothers. There was an opportunity, however, for anyone who was bright enough to win a scholarship to St. Mel's College in Longford as one was made available annually and was awarded to the pupil who obtained the highest marks in the entry exam. I was honoured and delighted when Master Moran selected myself and one other boy from my class to sit the exam which was held in Mohill.

I was even more delighted when, some weeks later, I learned that I had won the scholarship! It would entitle me to attend St. Mel's without having to pay the necessary fees for education, board and lodging. Sadly, it was not to be. When the letter came from St. Mel's to my parents, outlining that while the basic cost of my education would be covered, there was a long list of items which I would need to supply myself, books, clothes, shoes etc. Mother surveyed the list and did the calculation. There was no possible way that they could afford to send me. The scholarship was declined and the place went to the boy who had done second best in the exam.

Disappointed as I was, I put it behind me and convinced myself that I wouldn't have liked it anyway! That said, in subsequent years, I never felt that I had missed out or that my lack of educational qualifications held me back in any respect. In some ways, I almost feel that what I achieved was even more worthy due to the fact that I didn't have the advantages that someone who came from a more affluent background would have had.

My formal school education ended when I was three months shy of my fourteenth birthday. My mother's father, who had moved in with us, was seriously ill with cancer and Mother needed help minding him. It was hard work but I was there with him to the very end. He had trouble breathing and I gently lifted him up to see if he could catch his breath. A few minutes later he had passed. I had heard about the "rattle of death" and it was then that I truly understood what people meant when they had spoken of it. His whole body trembled just before he went; I knew exactly what was happening and what it meant. He was only 66 years of age which, these days, is considered young but back then, in 1938, he was described at his wake as living to be "a good age".

After my Grandfather's passing, I didn't return to school but instead continued to help Mother around the house while my brother Sean helped to plant the crops in the fields. I knew that I was too ambitious to be content staying at home on the farm, so during this time I kept my eyes peeled for employment. One day, my attention was drawn to an advertisement in *The Independent*, whereby a shopkeeper in Maynooth, Kildare, was looking for a retail assistant. He was offering a three year apprenticeship with bed and meals provided but there would be no pay. Instead the lucky applicant would pay a deposit of fifty pounds for the privilege of working for him! Having given the matter due consideration, I concluded that yes, the retail trade might be where my future lay and duly sent off my application. I wrote to him explaining that my family did not have fifty pounds but that I was eager, reliable and a hard worker. I was delighted when soon after, I learned that despite the lack of the fifty pounds, he was agreeable to giving me the position.

Leaving home for the first time I took one of several buses which eventually landed me in Maynooth on 1 September 1939, my first day on the job. The shop was a busy general grocery store that also sold newspapers and petrol. I worked alongside a boy from Belfast who was two years older than me. We were called at half seven every morning and the shop opened until at eight o'clock. Myself and my colleague would take it in turn to have our twenty minute breakfast. The shop remained open until eight o'clock at night, except Wednesdays when it closed at one in the afternoon. That was our half-day but instead of being free to spend it as we pleased, instead we had to spend it in the shop weighing out sugar into bags. Then we had to walk the family's two cocker spaniels while our boss had a rest. On Sundays the shop opened from eight in the morning to one in the afternoon. After lunch I walked the dogs again which at least meant that I got to escape from the place for a while.

Of course because I was only beginning to learn how the business worked, I made mistakes but unfortunately for me Richard, my co-worker, wasn't in the least bit understanding regarding my lack of experience. On my third day I sold a gallon of paraffin oil to a woman but only charged her for half a gallon. It was Richard who brought the mistake to my attention and threatened to report me if I didn't fix it. I took the price of the missing half gallon from my own purse and handed it over to him. I repeated the same mistake but this time it was butter, I sold a pound of butter for the price of half a pound. Once again Richard collected the balance from me.

I was far from happy, with no friends and nothing to do aside from working and walking the dogs. Richard was never less than unfriendly and my employer was no better. Moreover, I was homesick and missed my family greatly. Realising I did not want to be a shopkeeper after all and had made a huge mistake, I took to writing home, begging for money so that I could take the bus back to Leitrim. I sent off the first letter but heard nothing in reply. I sent off a second letter and still heard nothing. How could I have known that my mother was extremely proud of her son's apprenticeship with a Maynooth shopkeeper and had told all the neighbours about my new-found status? My father had not wanted me to leave but she was delighted, believing that once I had learned my trade, I would never be out of a job. I learned afterwards that following my departure, Mother had advised all her neighbours that Michael was 'away to be a Shop Boy' and did her best to give them regular updates on the wonderful progression of my career which was very much at odds with the version she was getting in my written entreaties.

I was growing increasingly desperate as my pleas to my mother were not yielding the desired response. My final attempt in securing my release involved a pitiful appeal, describing how my situation was having a dreadful impact on my state of health. 'Things are so bad Mother', I wrote, 'that I've lost the high colour in my cheeks.' As Mother had always lauded her middle son's lovely healthy complexion, I reckoned that if that didn't do it, nothing would!

Finally my third letter resulted in a postal order, the price of the bus ticket. I don't think I will ever forget my delight on opening that envelope. Ignoring my responsibilities I immediately ran out to the Post Office and cashed it. I ran all the way back to the shop and packed my suitcase. My boss was behind the counter and without so much as a "by your leave", I told him I was going home. He was disgusted, 'you stupid boy! Walk out that door today and as God is my witness, I tell you, you'll never make anything of yourself!' I didn't care. All I knew was that I was free. That shop had felt like a jail and now the world had suddenly exploded in size again. I walked out beaming and boarded the bus home. It was truly a most wonderful feeling.

Back home my mother was slightly embarrassed at the abrupt end to my shop-keeping career. For about two weeks after my return, any time the neighbours came by I was told to hide out in the parlour until they left. When she considered herself finally recovered from the embarrassment of the situation, she steeled herself to 'go public' and embarked on circulating the story of my supreme unhappiness under unendurable conditions at the mercy of a mean and cruel boss. It was the best excuse she could come up for her delinquent son.

***

There were many great characters in Cloone itself and the surrounding areas many of whom were the protagonists in some humorous tales about situations in which they had found themselves. As the years unfolded such characters and their stories became almost legendary in the annals of local folklore. The following is a story I wrote some years ago about one such character.

For Sale by Public Auction

Nuckey McDaid was a fifty-one year old confirmed bachelor. A small, miserable looking man, he lived alone on a small farm consisting of fifteen acres of poor land in Lissdo, in the parish of Coolmore, in South Leitrim. Home was a small, three-roomed thatched cottage that stood three quarters of a mile back from the road, down a crooked dirt track that was overgrown with bushes and briars. The nearest shop was a four mile walk.

For years Nuckey tried his best to make a living on his farm but the land was just too bad to yield much of anything. He was the last in a long line of McDaids who had lived and worked in Lissdo. His grandfather and father had somehow managed to survive on the land and rear big families so Nuckey couldn't help feeling like a dismal failure. The alternative was to sell everything and emigrate but how could he betray his father and all he had worked for? In any case what was he qualified for? Plenty were taking the boat to England in search of work but what would he be fit for, with no trade and little education? He could probably pick up some work from a local farmer but the real work would involve trying to get paid. Come Saturday evening he might be told there was no change and be asked what mass he'd be at the next day. The farmer would promise to see him at the church to pay him what was due but invariably they would miss one another, at the farmer's instigation. It was a common enough occurrence at that time.

The other problem was his neighbours. What would they say if they heard he had been forced to sell up and go to England? Some would be genuinely sorry for him while others would be genuinely delighted at the opportunity to buy his land on the cheap. And then there was Bear's Mouth Moore, his next door neighbour and arch enemy. His land bordered Nuckey's. If he bought the farm all he would have to do was break a gap in the fence and he'd have a nice holding for himself.

They had been enemies for years, fighting over things like broken fences, or who had the right of way to the well and to the bit of cut away bog. One summer Nuckey's cow broke into Bear's Mouth's meadow and was happily working her way through his hay when he spied her. Enraged at the transgression, he grabbed a spade and chased her back to the road, whacking her every so often on the rump. Nuckey arrived and an actual fight broke out. They rolled around the dirt in deadly combat. At some point Nuckey took Bear's Mouth down with a vicious kick to the lower belly. Fearing that he would lose to the smaller man he became desperate enough to grab the spade once more and this time bash Nuckey twice over the head. He went in for a third hit but was restrained by another neighbour, Crooger Hurley, who tore the weapon out of his hands. 'For God's sake!' roared Crooger, 'Will ye have a bit of sense and act like a pair of Christians!' He helped Nuckey to his feet. Blood was pouring from a deep cut at his right temple and a similar cut just above his left ear.

'You saw what happened, didn't you?' Nuckey demanded. 'He murdered me with the spade and you're my witness.' Not wishing to become involved Crooger shook his head, 'No, I didn't see a thing. I was looking down at the lake when I bumped into the two of you'. Nuckey ignored the slight, 'Well, I'm off to the guards. This time he has gone too far!'

Sergeant James Gallagher was the officer in charge in Coolmore. A practical and kind-hearted man, he was very popular throughout the parish. Nuckey appeared in front of him, his trousers torn and, like his shirt, covered in blood. 'In the name of God, what happened to you?' he asked. Nuckey wiping blood from his cheek answered, 'I was murdered, Sergeant, and I want you to arrest the man responsible.'

'Of course, of course!' said the Sergeant, immediately guessing much of what had happened, 'Come on in.' He seated Nuckey at a table, fetched a basin of warm water, some soap and a cloth and washed the victim's face as best as he could. Next he sat down opposite him with his pen and notepad, 'Right, Nuckey, I need to take a statement. Tell me who assaulted you and as many details as you can remember about the incident.'

There was silence. Sergeant Gallagher looked up at Nuckey who was staring at the pen that was ready to take down every word he uttered. 'Nuckey, I'm waiting. Who did this to you?' Nuckey came to: 'You want me to tell you who assaulted me?' The Sergeant nodded, 'That's right! Just give me a name; it's as simple as that'. Nuckey was horrified, 'Sergeant Gallagher, no disrespect intended but you know me for a long time now. I was never an informer and never will be. It's your job to find out who did this because – as long as your arsehole looks to the ground – you won't find it out from me!' With that, Nuckey straightened his cap, turned on his heel and left the Sergeant in stunned silence.

As the days passed Nuckey thought long and hard about his future, confusing himself until he felt unable to make a decision either way. Should he sell? Should he take his chances in England despite the fact he had no confidence he would be able to find a job? What if he was left with absolutely nothing? What if he was left with nowhere to call home?

It was now the first week of August and quite a few boys and girls were home from England for their annual holiday. They were all well-dressed and the boys, at least, had money to buy drinks for their former neighbours in the bars of Coolmore. Nuckey enjoyed the occasional pint and arrived into Kennedy's pub about 8.30pm. There he bumped into Barney Crowley. Barney had grown up about a half mile from Nuckey's farm. He came from a large family, with seven brothers and four sisters, and they had all emigrated, some to Canada, America and New Zealand. Meanwhile Barney and Joe, his twin, headed to Birmingham where they found work on the building sites. Nuckey was glad to see him.

'You'll have a pint?' asked Barney. 'Aye, at least!' said Nuckey and was much impressed when Barney told Kathleen Connolly, the friendly barmaid, to keep the eight pence change. Four pints later Nuckey had confided all his financial fears in Barney who told him not to worry, 'You would have no problem getting a job in Birmingham. They are mad for Irish fellows who aren't afraid of hard work. The wages are good and there is plenty of overtime. And if you wanted to work Sundays they pay double time.' Barney searched his pockets and then brought out his last pay slip. The gross amount, which included two weeks overtime and holiday pay, was eight-two pounds and seventy-six pence.

Nuckey's eyes widened at this immense total. He wouldn't make that amount in six months on the farm. No more worrying and fretting, it was now perfectly obvious what he should do. 'Christ, Barney, am I glad I met you tonight! I'd be a bloody fool to continue the slavery at Lissdo when there is such good money to be made in England. I should have gone over years ago.'

Barney slapped him on the shoulder in agreement, 'I'll tell you what I'll do. My gaffer is a Mayo man and I get on very well with him. I'll give you the address. Look me up as soon as you get off the boat and I'll get you sorted.'

For the first time in a long time Nuckey was excited and full of hope about his future. He cycled home free of the weight of indecision. It was easy now that he knew what he had to do, sell everything he owned and set sail for John Bull's land. He could return to Leitrim when he had made enough money to buy a small pub. Surely that was where money was to be made in Ireland.

The next morning he cycled over to Mohill to meet with Joe Farrelly, the genial auctioneer. Nuckey told him he wanted to sell the farm and furnished Joe with all the details he needed to do his job. When they were finished Joe told Nuckey that the farm would be advertised that very week in the *Leitrim Observer*.

The paper was published on a Thursday and was delivered to Pat Manning's shop in Coolmore on Friday, in time for the weekend. Nuckey was possibly the first to buy it that particular week. He turned the pages until he reached the 'Sale and Auction' section whereupon he read:

For Sale by Public Auction

I have been favoured with instruction by Patrick McDaid, Esquire, of Lissdo, Coolmore, to offer for sale, by public auction, his farm, at three o'clock, Friday, 25 August 1942, his valuable holding consisting of fifteen statute acres, two roods and three square perches, or thereabouts.

Access to the holding is from the nearby main road, via a lovely winding avenue, bounded on either side by a strong, mature hedge. The land is well watered and fenced with a never-ending supply of spring water and tubbary rights.

By a generous application of farmyard and artificial manures over the years, the land is in good heart and renowned for its fattening qualities. The holding, which commands a panoramic view of lovely Sliabh An Iarainn, is conveniently situated to church, school, shops, post office, creamery etc.

There is a magnificent dwelling house maintained in immaculate condition throughout. Convenient to the house is a wide range of out-offices, with byre accommodation for eight cows, stables for two horses and an open shed for young livestock, pig sty and fowl house.

Any person anxious to acquire a really first class holding is strongly advised to attend this auction, as seldom does property of its equal come on the market.

Terms – 5% auctioneer's fees.

J. Boland & Co., Solicitors, Mohill, having carriage of sale.

Joe Farrelly, M.I.A.A., West Street, Mohill.

There is an old and true saying that "paper never refused ink". A stranger reading that advertisement would quite naturally conclude that Nuckey was selling a valuable and desirable piece of property. The neighbours, however, could not be fooled. The facts were thus, Nuckey's farm was convenient to no place, standing at the back of beyond. You ran the risk of losing an eye on that winding avenue, such was the quality and quantity of the thorn bushes. As for the land's "fattening qualities", it wouldn't feed snipe. True, there was an abundance of water and tubbery rights –plentiful commodities in South Leitrim – however, there was no fencing. The 'magnificent dwelling house' was ready to fall down while a lean-to thatched construction at the back of the dwelling house was the sum total of the wide range of out-offices.

One person was very impressed with the exaggerated attributes of the Lissdo farm, the one person who knew better than anyone else what was on offer. On Monday morning Nuckey presented himself back at the auctioneer's office to tell Joe Farrelly that the farm was no longer for sale. In answer to Joe's bewilderment, Nuckey explained, 'To tell you the truth, when I read the advertisement it made me realise what a great place I had after all. I'd be a fool to even think about selling it.' With that he took his leave of the bemused auctioneer and headed back to his beloved Lissdo.

Local Defence Force (LDF)

My brother Seán joined the Local Defence Force, the forerunner of today's FCA, (An Fórsa Cosanta Áitiúil), in January 1940. It was set up as a response to the outbreak of World War II and was a combination of a defence force and a police force. Volunteers from every locality signed up to keep the twenty-six counties safe, reporting any hostility or breach of security to the controlling authority, An Garda Síochána. The older men, the auxiliary force, performed patrols while the younger members were trained in the use of fire arms.

Superintendent Willie Joe McConville was the commanding officer in Mohill which was about five miles away from where I lived. Known as the Garda District Officer, he had in his charge five sub-districts: Mohill, Cloone, Carrigallen, Farnaught and Dromod. He visited Cloone every Tuesday night to supervise the training. I badly wanted to join, as did my friends, Andy McKeon and Dan Dillon but, alas, we were rejected by our local sergeant because we were too young. Seán arrived home from training one evening and left his rifle propped up against the dresser. Unable to resist it, I picked it up causing my brother to roar, 'Put that down! You're not trained in the use of fire arms!' It was humiliating to say the least. More than anything, I yearned to be a part of that elite group of combatants !

Following three weeks of training, the Superintendent reckoned that the Cloone branch was ready to march in public. Up to now they had practiced their drills in a yard, hidden behind a corrugated fence. My friends and I took to sitting on a wall across the road, and could only hear the Superintendent call out his orders to the company. We waited impatiently for the big moment when the door was opened to allow McConville's fusiliers to troop outside. They were in civilian attire, still to receive their uniforms, but looked smart in their lines, not that I was impressed of course, trying to convince myself that if I couldn't be a part of it then it really wasn't anything special. Instead, when they marched outside I took the opportunity, as a sulky reject, to cause a bit of mayhem, much to the delight of my two friends.

The company came through the gate and the Superintendent called out in a shrill voice, 'Company left wheel!' Without thinking I imitated his tone and shouted, 'Company right wheel!' Naturally this caused confusion in the ranks with half the men turning one way while the rest of their colleagues found themselves facing them in utter confusion. My friends and I doubled over with laughter until we realised that we had been well and truly caught. Superintendent McConville came striding towards us, bellowing at the top of his voice, 'Who said that?' Not one of the three of us was able to make a reply. Looking at us in turn he rounded on me, 'It was you! I can tell by the glowing shame on your face.' Blushing fiercely, it was futile to deny the accusation, 'Yes, Sir. Sorry, Sir!' He puffed out his chest and shouted, 'I've a good mind to throw you all in the cells and let you cool your heels. Now, off home with the lot of you, this instant!' We ran as fast as we could before he had a chance to carry out his threat.

To fast forward a little, it so happened that many years later, in 1966, I was transferred to Drogheda, as Superintendent, where my Chief Superintendent was none other than the same Willie Joe McConville. We got to chatting and he asked me where I was from. When I said Cloone he regaled me about the nine pleasant years he had spent stationed there, telling me that his greatest achievement had been the setting up the Cloone branch of the LDF. As I stood there he suddenly remembered that the first public showing of his company had been upset by a little chiseller who shouted out opposing orders to his own. I smiled, 'What did you do to him?' My Chief shrugged, 'Why, I gave him a right telling off and ran him home!' His expression was an absolute picture when I confessed to being that little chiseller!

My wish to join the LDF came true a few short months later when a new garda came to the village. I went to him to make my application and when giving my particulars, added the required years to my age – of which he was blissfully ignorant – and duly received my uniform and rifle. I was promoted to Corporal after three months and no ordinary corporal at that since I was given the impressive title of Intelligence Officer. My first task was to carry out an investigation of all lakes and rivers in the district of Cloone to make sure they had not been manipulated in any way by Germans submarines! Yes, it was a complete waste of time but I had my orders and faithfully carried out my research. Having spent many hours surveying the marine life of the said lakes and rivers, I returned a negative verdict which was no surprise to anyone.

My mettle, as a Corporal was to be tested when, in October 1941, I received the news that British Army troops were advancing from

Enniskillen to take over ports in the Republic. All LDF members were put on alert and a plan was put into effect to ensure that the incursion would be averted. Armed men were to be placed at various strategic junctions to await the Army's advance. I had six volunteers under my command and was working out how best to deploy them so as to thwart the advancing forces. In the group of six, were two brothers, Sean and Robbie Morrow, who made up for in enthusiasm what they lacked in experience of bloody combat!

Having decided to take charge of three junctions, I detailed my men where to take up their positions. I allocated Sean Morrow and another volunteer to the junction of Kiltyfea Cross while, his brother Robbie's posting was to Costello's Cross, again with a second volunteer by his side. My remaining two volunteers were sent elsewhere. My men were duly despatched and only about ten minutes had passed when I spotted Robbie in the distance on the return journey to me.

As he got nearer, I could see he had tears in his eyes. When I asked him why he was back so soon, he replied, 'You have to send me to Kiltyfea Cross.' Confused, I reminded him that Kiltyfea was already being manned by two volunteers which I believed was a sufficient number to see off the approaching enemy. Robbie grew increasingly distressed. 'Michael you don't understand. Sean is at Kiltyfea Cross. If I'm going to die, I want to die with my brother, so that's why I have to go!' I assured poor Robbie that he truly was in no imminent danger and eventually he returned to Costello's Cross, ready and willing to lay down his life for his country. Needless to say, having spent a very boring few hours lying in a ditch observing nothing more threatening than the odd passing bicycle and stray dog, he was home in good time to join his brother Sean for their supper!

On the occasion of the same emergency, another young volunteer, Sean Bohan, (of the same name as my own brother, but no relation), had taken up position that night at the bottom of our vegetable garden. He had dug himself a 'fox hole' in which he had taken shelter and from where he could keenly observe the approach of any unwelcome forces while at the same time remaining out of view of the enemy. Aware of his presence, Mother was greatly concerned about Sean's well-being and worried that he might be getting cold and hungry, even though he had only been on duty for about twenty minutes. I tried to explain to her that it really wasn't advisable for her to be running down to check on him repeatedly while simultaneously offering to sustain his strength, by bringing him cups of tea and home-made brack.

It was fortunate that she was persuaded to abandon her visits to Sean's post, as not long afterwards, Captain Devine from Mohill rode into view on his motorbike. He had come to inspect the post to assure himself that all was as it should be. Emerging from his den, Sean immediately stood to attention, saluting his superior officer and ready to answer any questions which would be asked of him, (with the obvious exception of the matter of breaks for tea and brack). Having firstly established the volunteer's name and rank and obviously impressed by Sean's apparent capability and enthusiasm, Captain Devine continued, 'Volunteer Bohan, what types of grenades are you firing tonight?' With not a moment's hesitation, Sean replied, 'Turnips Sir.' It was true. In theory the LDF senior ranks were supposed to make available actual hand grenades to the volunteers but I can honestly say that there were very few amongst the ranks that had ever even seen one, never mind actually have one as part of our ammunition. Not to be impeded by such a minor issue, volunteers then assembled an assortment of whatever life threatening weapons they could lay hands on, but it was only Sean who had appreciated the lethal potential of the common or garden turnip !

In May 1942 the army set up a training camp on Lord Kilbracken's estate, Killegar House, in Carrigallen, which was located on the border of Cavan and Leitrim. On joining the LDF I was delighted to be able to go camping with my military colleagues. We slept in tents on the banks of the River Erne. Food was Spartan to say the least. Our main meal consisted of a cup of tea with two slices of leathery bread that had been briefly touched by a spoonful of jam. My friends and I took to walking into Killashandra every evening, for the week we were there, to avail of a much more appetising alternative meal for two shillings.

The leader of our company was Paddy McNiff who was a bit of joke for us, though he never knew that. Whenever he had to sign his name he always made sure to write, "BA (Bachelor of Arts)",after it. He had been to college and obviously wanted people to know this. He further exhibited his higher education every time he opened his mouth. Paddy never used simple language when he could throw in big words to impress his audience.

One of our training exercises saw us pitted against the army. We were to head out at six o'clock to find them before they could locate us and take them as our prisoners. Paddy was determined we'd prove ourselves superior to the army. I remember it as a dark and wet morning. Our scouts, who had been sent out to locate the army contingent, reported back that they were taking shelter in a building on the estate. Paddy was delighted, reckoning it would make it that much easier to surprise them. He led the way, urging us to be as quiet as possible. One of our lads had a keen dislike for Paddy. As soon as we were in sight of where the army boys were hiding he strode a few feet away from us and let out three big whooping cheers. Naturally, the army came running immediately and took us all in one fell swoop. Paddy was beside himself with rage, shouting out language that one would not have expected to hear from the mouth of a BA holder – with not a three-syllabled word in sight.

There was a young corporal called Tommy who had a dreadful fear of rats. Of course if one is going to attend a week long camping spree with a bunch of young, free-spirited fellows, the wisest course would be not to mention any personal fears or weaknesses. One evening, following a particularly exhausting day, Tommy turned in early. While he was fast asleep in his tent beside the river, one of the others caught a frog, sneaked in to where Tommy lay sleeping soundly and gently placed it in the fold at the bottom of his trouser leg. He went back outside, grabbed a stick and started shouting, 'Rat! Rat!' Poor Tommy jumped up and came running out, 'What's wrong?' Of course the frog was disturbed by all of the commotion and on feeling something cold and soft against his skin Tommy naturally assumed it was the aforementioned rat. He screamed, turned and with an impressive jump dived into the river. As you can imagine it proved a popular topic of conversation for the rest of the week.

1944: An Garda Síochána

In January 1944 an advertisement appeared in all the national newspapers; An Garda Síochána were inviting young men to join the force. Specifically they were asking for recruits aged between nineteen and twenty-three years of age, with a minimum height of five feet nine inches and a chest measurement of thirty nine inches. I don't remember having an ambition, at that time, about any particular career, all I know is that when I read that advert I knew that I fulfilled all the physical requirements and didn't think too far beyond that. I immediately applied.

I cycled the fifty-five miles to Athlone to take the Garda examination on Ash Wednesday in February 1944. It was a long day; we took our seats at 10am, with a break for lunch, and didn't finish until 5pm that evening. To my delight I passed and midway through October I was called for an interview and medical examination at the Garda Headquarters in the Phoenix Park.

We were taken in groups of ten to the Garda Depot hospital to be examined by Doctor Ellis, the Garda Surgeon. There we were met by a tall, distinguished looking gentleman who wore a white coat with a thermometer sticking out of his breast pocket. Naturally we all assumed he was the surgeon. In fact he was Jim Donnelly, a hospital orderly who loved to play jokes on anyone who strayed across his path. Accordingly, he allowed us to continue addressing him as Doctor Ellis.

Part of the physical examination involved the presenting of a urine sample. Joe Kelly, a fellow recruit, handed his sample to "Doctor Ellis" – that is, Jim – who shook it gravely from side to side and eyed it carefully. 'Young man', said Jim, 'I'd say your father is a sergeant in the force'. Joe gushed, 'Why, yes he is, Sir! Do you know him?' The "doctor" shook his head, 'No, I don't, but I always know a sergeant's son's urine when I see it!'

After the examination Joe sat with us for a while, we were allowed coffee and biscuits. He told us that he had fought in the Civil War and explained that he could never sit near a fire because of the amount of "Black and Tan" bullets that were embedded in his backside. As our eyes widened he explained that if the bullets got warm the lead would melt into his blood circulation and kill him 'stone dead'. How he didn't burst out laughing at our worried expressions, I'll never know. We were a captive audience and no mistake. In due course I was informed that I had passed both the medical exam and the interview. My path to a career in An Garda Siochana was clear!

A few weeks before I was due to begin my training at the Depot in Dublin, I suffered from a severe pain in my right side and went to the family doctor in Leitrim to see what the problem was. He diagnosed an inflamed appendix. He sent me to the only hospital in Leitrim, Manor Hamilton Hospital, to have it removed. When my friends heard about my forthcoming operation they assured me that I had nothing to fear because Surgeon O'Carroll, my surgeon, had had his hands and medical instruments blessed by the Pope and furthermore he had never lost a patient on the table. Now, he may have lost patients after they left his table but, in the opinion of my friends, that did not count.

Hospitals back then were very different from the clinically, sterile, patient centred facilities we speak of today. Conditions were appalling and patients were treated like errant school children. My ward, containing twenty-five beds, with one toilet between us, was supervised by 'Matron'. She was a Reverend Mother, a somewhat large lady with an extremely red face and she was relentlessly tough on her nurses. In those days the nurses, aside from taking care of the patients, were responsible for all the cleaning and general house-keeping on the wards, so needless to say, they were always run off their feet.

After an operation a patient was expected to spend the entire day sitting up in bed with arms folded over the top of the sheets and do nothing else for fear they would burst their stitches. In those days you could smoke in bed, but only until lights out at ten o'clock. Thankfully I wasn't a smoker at the time. At ten o'clock Matron patrolled the wards to make sure that both lights and cigarettes had been extinguished. One night she came into my ward and detected a whiff of smoke. She went from bed to bed enquiring if anyone was smoking, each reply was the same, 'No, Reverend Mother', until she reached John Joe Crilly's bed, the culprit. He was addicted to Woodbine cigarettes and was hiding one beneath his blankets. Matron asked in a shrill voice, 'Have you a cigarette, Crilly?' His reply was immediate, 'Christ, yes, Sister. Do you want one?'

He received a ferocious telling off for his generosity!

1945: Garda Headquarters, Dublin

I was officially recruited to An Garda Siochana on 16 November 1945, and was one of seventy-two recruits that moved into Garda Headquarters, the Depot, in the Phoenix Park, for five months of training. It was a huge building, which was formerly the HQ of the RIC (Royal Irish Constabulary). We slept fourteen to a room on biscuit thin mattresses and beneath three grey blankets that did not exactly smell as though they had been freshly, if ever, laundered. For the first two weeks there was no hot water. Keeping clean required a stoic determination to ignore the winter temperatures. Our weekly pay amounted to the princely sum of two pounds and ten shillings.

The days did not vary in content. Our seven o'clock wake-up call was a trumpet "Reveille". This is the typical way to wake military personnel at sunrise and can be played on the trumpet, bugle or even pipes. Its name comes from the French word, *"reveille"*, ("wake up"). We got out of bed, washed, dressed and headed out into the square for the "Check Parade". I could never figure out the purpose of this exercise unless it was meant to be a form of early morning punishment. All it entailed was the Sergeant calling out our names and us answering as Gaeilge, 'Anseo!' We were then dismissed and retired to the Mess Room for a breakfast of porridge, bread and tea. The bread wasn't always buttered especially during the war years when butter was rationed.

Our first session began at nine o'clock. It was either a class on Police Duties in English, or Irish, or else we were back out in the square doing yet another infernal drill. We spent many, many hours drilling and parading around the square. It seemed a bit of a waste of time since the only time we paraded anywhere was to mass on Sunday with the band accompanying us with marching tunes. People would stop to watch the show which I don't doubt was impressive.

Dinner was at served at one o'clock and more often than not, the only offering was stew. The result of all those stews over those five months resulted in my life-long hatred of that particular dish. After dinner there was more of the same drilling or classes. Tea was – hopefully – buttered bread and cups of tea. Once that was out of the way we were free to do what we wanted as long as we were back in our dormitory at eleven o'clock.

I must admit that I was less than impressed with the training we received. It was mainly instruction in formation in drill, umpteen times around the Depot yard, (an exercise we referred to as 'square bashing'), under the command of two drill sergeants, Sergeant Johnny Beale and Sergeant Jim McGrath. Both men had been drill sergeants in the British army and joined An Garda Síochána on its inception in 1922. As they had not been instructed to do otherwise, they continued to do what they had been doing with the army.

We had to buy our own timber kit boxes at a cost of five shillings that we kept our belongings in. Believe me, there was nothing worth stealing in any of them but one lad, John Nicholson, from Athlone, got himself a padlock for his box. Perhaps he felt his butter ration wasn't safe. As soon as he received his weekly supply, it was safely locked away in the kit box.

One morning Bertie McHugh and I were late getting out for the Check Parade, about three to four minutes in total but it was enough to convince us that it would be best if we simply reported sick instead of leaving ourselves open to a disciplinary charge. Later that day, about three o'clock, we were in our respective beds when a small, scraggly terrier dog arrived into our room. He looked hungry. Bertie had an idea, 'Wouldn't it be great if we could put him in John Nicholson's box'. I looked at him, 'But how? It's locked'. Bertie sat up, 'Sure, I'll just pick the lock!' Removing the small clip that was holding his cap badge in place, he did just that and placed the little dog inside.

There was no mistaking the sound of John rattling his keys on his return to the dormitory. He immediately crossed to his bed and did what he always did, which was to open his kit box and check on the contents. The dog's head popped up, its snout and nose greasy from the butter. Not surprisingly, John took a few paces back in surprise and then in utter confusion as to how the dog got into a locked box. His face was a picture of amazement. Giving up, he seized the dog and chased him down the stairs.

John had great faith in me so it was me that he came to, to ask if I had seen anyone interfering with his box. I replied, 'Well, I'm as much puzzled as you are, John. All I know is that at about three o'clock Bertie and I fell asleep so that must have been when the dog came into the room. But how on earth he got into the box is anybody's guess!'

The following Saturday John took himself off to Woolworth's for a bigger lock.

I'm afraid we did give poor John a hard time. He was quite homesick, more than the rest of us. Whenever my friend Joe Holden sang, "The Lights of Home", John's eyes would shine with tears. After tea his most frequent past-time was to walk to Aston Quay to meet the Athlone bus to see if anyone he knew was on it. He particularly hoped to meet Billy, who apparently was his best friend from back home and who, it seemed, spoke frequently of paying a visit to the 'Big Smoke'.

One evening he had a cold and had to forego his walk. I headed off to another part of town. When I came back I fibbed to John that I had been standing on Aston Quay to meet my cousin off the Athlone bus, 'When she got off the bus she introduced me to a fellow by the name of Barry Hines who, on hearing I was a recruit in the Depot, asked if I knew you. I told him I shared a room with you and he said that you both had been best friends for years and I was to give you his best regards'.

John's reply to this fabrication was to burst into genuine tears! I must admit to feeling a little guilty when I saw his upset, but on reminding myself of how precious he was about never sharing the contents of his kit box, my guilt subsided!

Sergeant McGrath also doubled as a first aid instructor. He lectured us regarding the procedure to be followed if a person had been injured in any kind of an accident. We learned that there were three vital steps that had to be taken to ensure the person survived:

1. Reassure the patient

2. Look for pain at or near the seat of injury

3. Give the patient either ice or thick gruel to suck

Pardon my language, but what utter bullshit. Whatever about the first two instructions, the idea of trying to locate either ice or gruel at the scene of an accident was beyond my comprehension. Needless to say, I never did manage to secure either item during the entire course of the numerous accidents I attended during my career.

The recruits were allowed to go out on alternative Saturday nights. Sometimes we would go to the céilí in the Recreation Hall at the Depot or else there were many other dancehalls to choose from around Parnell Square: the National Ballroom, the Galway Arms, the Irene Ballroom, the Teacher's Club and Conaghy's Hotel.

One Saturday night we headed over to the dance in the Teachers' Club, in Parnell Square, where I met an absolute beauty. She was about twenty years of age, tall, slim, blonde and very elegant. How lucky was I that she actually asked me to dance when the band called for "Ladies' Choice", whereby the women approached the men who had caught their eye. Her name was Mary Mullarkey, a Roscommon girl. I told her where I was from and that I was a guard in training at the depot. We danced together for ages that night and then I walked her home. She was living with her married sister on the North Circular Road, about five houses from the main entrance to the Phoenix Park. We agreed to meet the following Saturday at three o'clock to see the film "Gone with the Wind". I was over the moon with my very good fortune and spent the intervening days looking forward to my date with the lovely Mary.

Now I must return to the previous Saturday night when I had attended a dance at the Depot. The band started to play an old time waltz which was the signal for the men, who sat on one side of the room, to cross the floor to the other side, where the women were sitting, and pick a pretty girl to dance with. I was sitting beside my fellow recruit Dan Kennedy. As soon as the band struck up the waltz we both made a run for the same girl, the extremely attractive Theresa Hall. Dan got there first and Theresa got up happily to dance with him, leaving me in an awkward situation as I realised that the girl sitting next to her thought that I was coming to ask her up. With not a moment's hesitation, the girl, one Joan Beale, left her seat and walked towards me with her arms out, ready to dance. However, I did not fancy Joan Beale in the slightest and faced with all the options under duress, I panicked and did something absolutely rotten. I turned my back on her and returned to my seat. Apart from the fact it was downright rude it was also a downright stupid thing to do since it transpired that Joan's father was in fact none other than, Sergeant Beale, my drill sergeant.

The Thursday after that we had been, as usual, drilling in the square for a good forty-five minutes when we received the order, 'Company Halt!', ' Company Stand at Ease!' or 'Company Stand Easy!' In other words we were free to relax and chat amongst ourselves for a few minutes. During the break I told a joke to Joe Holden and Tom Mullarkey, causing them to laugh out far too loudly for the Sergeant's liking. Unfortunately I cannot remember the joke now but I do know that I did not laugh myself. Nevertheless Sergeant Beale confronted me, took my name and registered number and the next day, Friday, I was paraded before the Depot Commandant, Chief Superintendent Casserly, charged with discreditable conduct for laughing on parade. Sergeant Beale gave his evidence, which was very brief, and then I spoke up to defend myself and apologise. 'Shut up, you!' roared the Commandant, 'You have no right of audience here. Charge proved!' And that was that. My sentence was handed out; I would be confined to the Depot all weekend.

Needless to say, there couldn't have been a worse weekend for my punishment to have been meted out. All I could think of was Mary Mullarkey and the date that now wasn't going to happen. The romance was over before it had even begun.

After lunch I had to report to the Sergeant in the Guard Room, which was just at the entrance of the Depot, who fitted me out with a pair of blue overalls, with the letters BOW, (Board of Works), inscribed on the back. It was a far cry from my usual uniform and wasn't exactly elegant. I was detailed to pick weeds and grass out from the cobble stones outside. Of course I had absolutely no way of communicating this change of plan to the prospective love of my life. At three o'clock, on Saturday afternoon, I was weeding miserably, knowing that she was nearby, waiting for me at the entrance to the Phoenix Park. Mary was no wallflower and, after ten minutes or so, got impatient enough to make her way to the Depot to find me. Well, when she saw me on my knees, digging out dirt from the stones, in my fetching blue overalls she flew into a rage. I jumped up to explain myself but she never gave me a chance. 'Liar!' she shouted. 'You told me you were a recruit-in-training but now I see that you're just a handy-man of some sort. Were you trying to pull a fast one on me?' And off she marched, never to be seen again.

With hindsight I think maybe she did me a good turn. I'm not sure I would have been able for such a feisty wife!

1945: Graduation

In actual fact there was no graduation, no party or fanfare to mark the conclusion of our five months of training and the passing of the examinations. What happened was simply this: the Chief of the Dublin Metropolitan Division turned up to pick twenty of us for duty throughout the district of Dublin. He was due at two o'clock and before he arrived we continued on with our drill and classes as normal.

At that time recruits had to be at least six feet in height to be admissible to the Dublin Metropolitan Police, (DMP). So, the Chief merely selected the tallest of the class. One of my friends was desperately hoping to be picked for a Dublin city station for the simple reason that he had never learned how to cycle a bike, a necessity for a rural police station. Anyone whose name was called out, including my friends and myself, were told to prepare ourselves for being transferred to our relevant stations the following morning. I don't think any of us had much to pack, aside from a few bits of clothes and of course, our kit boxes.

The next morning the twenty of us headed out into the transport yard where a covered lorry was waiting to take us to our destinations. A short while later my three best friends and I found ourselves standing in front of Kevin Street Station, our new home. Inside we were met by the Staff Sergeant's bully, or assistant, who was dressed in civilian attire so we did not realise he was a garda himself. He gave us our district numbers; this is how we would be referred to by our superiors in the future. I was 54A, Joe Holden was 68A, Con Lenihan was 103A and Tom Mullarkey was 59A. He also gave us our uniforms and the black capes which were standard issue back then.

We were then introduced to the Station Sergeant who told us that two of us would be reporting for duty at a quarter to six, the following morning. Joe nudged me and whispered, 'Ask him if you and I can come out together on the early relief'.

And so I did. 'Sir, would it be in order for 68A and I to come out on the early relief together?'

The Sergeant looked at me in disbelief, 'Good God Almighty! What's the job coming to when a red-arsed recruit, not five bloody minutes in the station is looking for concessions!'

Some concession, I thought, to have to get up at five o'clock in the morning. However, he did agree to my request.

The four of us would be sharing a dormitory room with twenty others. It was called the "Fifteen Acres" due to its massive size. Getting a good night's sleep would prove difficult what with fellows going out and returning to bed at different times, depending on their shifts. It was also difficult in the cold weather as the temperature in that room plunged whenever there was the slightest hint of a chill in the air. I remember patrolling the streets on cold nights and then returning to the dormitory, dreading the moment when I had to slide my shivering body beneath sheets that felt like ice in my hands.

We took our meals in the Mess Room, a large canteen that could seat fifty men, run by a woman who had previously cooked for the Christian

Brothers. She had three other women to help her. However the food in general proved to be a hit and miss affair, in that some meals were better than others. If you hit lucky you would leave the table heartily replete, if not you would stay hungry until the next mealtime.

There were three separate shifts: the morning shift started at six o'clock and finished at two o'clock; the day shift began at two o'clock and finished at ten o'clock, while the night shift began at ten o'clock and finished at six o'clock the following morning. The morning and day shifts were performed on alternate days while every three months you did an entire month of night shifts. We were going to be working seven days a week with four weeks annual leave, albeit the Sunday shift was a short one lasting four hours. Back then everyone went to mass, the guards included, attending in groups at the Carmelite Fathers Church on Whitefriar Street.

Because we were new recruits fresh out of the Depot we would be accompanied by mentors, senior guards, for the first weeks when we went out on "The Beat". That first morning I was paired up with the famous Jim Brannigan, who was known affectionately as "Lugs" on account of the generous size of his ears. He was a gentle giant and a complete gentleman. Our route comprised of just two streets, although they were extremely busy ones: Thomas Street and James Street. The day was spent patrolling them and then returning to the station for our relief, (break).

I marvelled at the way that Jim was treated by the stall holders, shop owners and the ordinary people on the street. Everyone seemed to know him and he greeted them all in turn, many by name. It was a great lesson in how to maintain good relations with the public. In fact I learned a lot about police work from Jim, especially regarding when to intervene in a situation. He gave me advice that I would never forget, to only ever get involved in something if I felt I could properly handle it by myself, otherwise I was to hang back and call for assistance.

We passed a group of young boys who began to cheekily chant 'Lugs! Lugs!' Jim caught one of them and marched him home to his mother. The mortified woman gave her son a clip around the ear and told him to apologise to Garda Brannigan for calling him names. Without thinking the boy said, 'Sorry, Lugs. I won't do it again!' Jim burst out laughing, the boy hardly knowing why.

On my second day I was accompanied by Chris Lang, another gentleman who briefed me on police duty in much the same way as Jim. I was thoroughly enjoying myself and, of course, completely relaxed being in the presence of two like-minded, practical and friendly senior guards.

My third day on the beat proved to be a little different when I found myself paired up with Garda Larry Jordan. A Kildare man, Larry was in his late fifties and a former member of the DMP. Somewhere along the line Larry had become rather weary of the job. To describe him as merely grumpy would be doing him an injustice. I think it would be more correct to say that the man had a grievance about being alive. He was miserable and had neither interest in nor time for young guards like myself.

Our beat was the colourful area around and including the Coombe. Larry and I walked along in silence except when he was insulting some poor creature for doing little or nothing at all to warrant such a greeting as, 'Watch where you're bloody going!' or 'What are you bloody staring at?' It seemed to me that he excelled in the practice of being deliberately nasty to the public.

At one point a group of men were standing outside Ryan's Pub. It was a glorious evening and no doubt influenced by Jim Brannigan and Chris Lang, I was anxious to cultivate good relations with the civilian population by being friendly with all and sundry. As we passed the men I smiled and said, 'Good evening, gentlemen. Isn't it beautiful weather, thank God!' They looked at me in utter amazement, making me doubt if any policeman had ever spoken to them before in such a friendly manner.

As we walked on Larry said, 'You shouldn't talk to those gougers'.

Thirsty for knowledge and ignorant of what he meant by a 'gouger', I asked him to explain to me what exactly constituted one.

'A gurrier!'

'And what is a gurrier?'

'A blood!'

'And what is a blood?'

'I told you, a gouger!'

I decided it would be an exercise in futility to pursue the matter further.

A few months later I managed to successfully pull the wool over Larry's eyes in order to get, or should I say win, a precious day off. During the month of night duty we were allowed one night off provided the regulation exigencies of the service permitted it, in other words provided there was enough staff on that particular night. Therefore, only one member of the night relief was allowed off at any one time. To avail of the leave you had to write to the Superintendent seeking his permission.

A couple of weeks earlier I had been best man at a friend's wedding. The couple had recently returned from their honeymoon in Galway and a huge party was being thrown for them in the bride's home on a Sunday night. I was invited and I very much wanted to be there. On the Thursday night I made my application on the "Leave Slip" to have the Sunday night free. As it turned out I wasn't the only one. Larry also wanted this particular night off. I anxiously wondered how this one was going to be resolved.

The Station Sergeant called the two of us together and told us, 'You both know the regulations. I can only release one from duty so settle it amongst yourselves'.

There was nothing for it but to plead with Larry, explaining to him that it was a wedding party and I was the best man and so forth. I begged him for the night. His answer was typically brief and blunt, 'No!'

Not prepared to give way so easily I tried again, 'Okay. Let's toss a coin for it'.

His repeated his first answer.

By this stage the rest of our colleagues, who were on nights that month, surrounded us amused, no doubt, by the temerity of a new recruit to challenge the authority of a man like Larry. The more senior of the crew urged Larry to agree to the coin toss. It took some time but eventually he agreed, albeit rather reluctantly.

I took a penny out of my pocket and said, 'Heads I win, Larry. Harp you lose'.

Not seeing anything wrong with this he didn't debate me, he simply watched that coin being tossed in the air and fall down on one side. Now, I cannot remember what side it fell on but it didn't matter, did it? What mattered was that Larry didn't understand that whichever way the penny fell I was the winner.

My Sunday night's leave was granted the next night. Dan Kelly, a senior guard, must have felt it necessary to crudely point out Larry's mistake to him, 'You're a fierce, ignorant shite, Larry! You let the young fella cod you'. Larry was mystified at the onslaught, saying, 'But didn't he win the toss?' Dan threw his eyes to Heaven, 'Of course he won because he couldn't have lost it and you're so thick you couldn't see that'.

In any case I went to the party and thoroughly enjoyed myself. As you can imagine my relationship with Larry did not exactly improve after my little trick on him.

1945: The Four Evangelists, Dublin

Four weeks out of training, I found myself patrolling Thomas Street when I bumped into my good friend Garda Joe Holden who himself was on duty on Meath Street, at the junction of Meath and Thomas Street and we stopped to chat. Our conversation was suddenly interrupted when a car that was coming out of Thomas Street and turning into Meath Street, collided with an on-coming bus. Since I was the senior recruit – my number was 9472 while Joe's was 9473 – I had to take charge of the investigation. Fortunately there was only material damage and no one was hurt.

Back at the station I reported the accident to the sergeant and he ordered me to prosecute the motorist for dangerous driving. In court I summoned both the bus driver and conductor as witnesses for the prosecution. Both Joe and I gave our account of what we had seen.

The defendant was represented by Trant McCarthy, a brilliant solicitor. After the evidence from the State concluded Mr McCarthy stood up and asked the Justice to dismiss the case on the grounds that two members of An Garda Síochána, who were professionally trained in observing events, had varied in their evidence while presenting their accounts for the court.

The Justice asked me, 'What do you have to say in reply to Mr McCarthy's submissions?'

Well, I hadn't a clue what to say. Indeed, it was news to me that we were supposed to be well trained in the powers of observation, apart from anything else. I thought for a few seconds and then I was suddenly inspired, possibly by the Holy Spirit Himself, to make my reply; 'Yes, Justice, it is correct to say that we varied in the evidence we gave but not on material matters. As you know, Justice, Matthew, Mark, Luke and John all wrote about the passion and crucifixion of Our Lord. They too varied in their account of the one event, but not on material matters. Despite the fact that they were divinely inspired they erred on minor matters. Surely then two members of An Garda Síochána, mere human beings, should be allowed to differ as long as they do not differ on material matters'.

I was most relieved to hear the Justice say, 'Well said, Garda!'

The defendant was duly fined a pound. That evening the headline on the front page of the *Evening Herald* read: "Two Gardaí and the Four Evangelists Win the Day in Court"

1945: Kevin Street : Inspecting A Licensed Premises

I was on my first month of night duty in July 1945. It began with a briefing at a quarter to ten in which we found out to which beat we had been assigned. We then headed out into the night, taking a thirty minute break at one o'clock the following morning. On this particular night I was accompanying one of our duty sergeants, Big Jim the Tank, who was well over six foot and something like twenty three stone. In spite of his considerable bulk, he seemed to glide gracefully along while I felt like a silly child beside him. He informed me that he wanted to show me how to inspect licensed premises to ensure that they were complying with the law. Since it was summer time all pubic houses should be closed at half-ten at night. Fifteen minutes after closing time the Sergeant said to me, 'Come on, we have our duty to do'.

We walked over to a popular pub, in the Coombe, J.G. O'Connor & Sons. As we approached the building it was obvious from the noise that there was a big crowd inside drinking away. I was delighted, anticipating issuing my first summonses. To my surprise the Sergeant knocked on the hall door, three large raps with the knocker. I had expected us to avail of the element of surprise and sneak in unannounced. The door was answered by Mr J.G O'Connor himself. He was a small man in his mid-sixties, a few strands of grey hair stuck across a bald patch, wearing a dickey bow and a blue and white apron. 'Good night, Sergeant!' he said, not so much as glancing my way. 'You'll be coming in?' he asked. The Sergeant nodded and we stepped inside. I took out my notebook preparing myself for name-taking and such like, hardly noticing that Mr O'Connor had led us to a snug. 'There you go, Sergeant, you'll have some peace here'. I stood confused until my Sergeant told me to sit down and relax. I sat down beside him and the hatch opened above our heads. It was Mr O'Connor again, 'You'll have a pint, Sergeant?'

'At least!', came the reply from my Sergeant.

In no time at all two frothy pints appeared and were handed into us. What on earth was going on? Why weren't we taking names and arresting the drinkers? I sat in silence, watching the Sergeant lift a pint to his lips and drink until he had emptied the glass. It was quite a feat. My own pint sat untouched. The Sergeant looked at it in surprise, 'Are you not drinking your pint, Sonny?'

'No, Sir,' I replied, 'I'm a pioneer.'

His eyes widened in what seemed to be genuine shock, 'In the name of God, what is a pioneer guard doing in a pub?' It was a good question and not the only one which was swimming around in my, by now very confused, head. What was I doing here? He knocked back my pint as swiftly as his own and then sank a third after that. I put my notebook back in my pocket when he declared, 'Right then, we'll be off!'

Outside he said to me, 'You saw how I inspected that premises. It's very important that the police have good relations with the public and the publicans. And that's what I was doing, lad.'

I completely disagreed but kept that to myself. In fact I was extremely disappointed at his behaviour, especially in front of a new recruit. He bade me to continue my beat by myself, 'Go on with you, now!' He went back into the pub and I headed up the Coombe feeling not a little frustrated. A crowd had come out of another pub and I could hear a strange noise, like a tap was running somewhere. Well, I could not believe my eyes when I saw women openly answering the call of nature at the side of the pub. This was it; I was going to make up for the last hour or so and do some proper police work. I approached the first woman, tipped her on the shoulder and exclaimed, 'You cannot do that here, Ma'am. It is an offence!' She roared at me, 'Take your bog hands of me, Culchie boy! What do you want me to do, spit it out like the cuckoo?'

I turned and quickly walked on, a wiser and humbler man while at the same time pondering the merits of any of the training I had received in the Depot. It most certainly hadn't prepared me for any of what I had just encountered that evening.

1945: Priorities in Kevin Street

Pre-1922 Ireland was policed by two police forces. Dublin, the capital, was under the jurisdiction of the Dublin Metropolitan Police, (DMP), whose wages were paid by Dublin Corporation, while the rest of Ireland was policed by the Royal Irish Constabulary, (RIC).

I remember on one occasion looking at an RIC Directory which made for the most interesting reading. Only the sons of gentlemen were allowed to join. Their apprenticeship lasted for three years, as cadets, before being promoted to the rank of officer. The highest rank available for an ordinary "Joe Soap" was that of Head Constable, akin to an Inspector in An Garda Síochána.

There were also two short paragraphs dealing with admission into the

DMP which read thus:

> *Young men anxious to join the DMP must have a minimum height of six feet in stocking feet and 39" across the chest.*

> *While reading and writing are not essential qualifications for admission to the DMP, nevertheless young men anxious to join would be well advised to have some modicum of instruction in these disciplines.*

Tony Kirwan was one of my colleagues in Kevin Street. A native of Connemara, he was fluent in Irish but had a poor knowledge of the English language.

Easter Monday night meant double beats around the Coombe area owing to the male population of the Liberties giving up drink for Lent and then, with the money they had saved, heading out to the Fairyhouse Races on the Monday before returning home that evening to drink the rest of their money away. Garda Kelly and I were on night duty in the area at ten o'clock and we had a busy night, arresting eleven rowdy individuals before one o'clock the next morning, the charges ranging from malicious damage to drunk and disorderly assaults.

Other guards on their beat had also arrested a similar number of prisoners so the station was packed since most of the prisoners had been accompanied by their protesting wives. The noise was fierce and the fighting tremendous. The floor was awash with blood and we did our best to calm down men who were determined to finish the battles started before their arrests. We were rapidly running out of cells as we couldn't put the fighters together so we had to process some there and then before trying to find room for them in other stations nearby.

In the midst of all this mayhem a decent looking, well-dressed gentleman arrived at the reception desk with a worried expression. Managing to ignore the fisticuffs and the yelling that was going on around him he went up to the hatch at the Station's Sergeant's Office and reported that his budgerigar, who answered to the name of Joe, had escaped from his cage. The Sergeant, a former member of the DMP, ordered Garda Tony

Kirwan to get a statement from him. Kirwan got a pencil and paper and proceeded to take the complainant's statement. He interrupted the Sergeant to ask, 'What is a budgerigar?'

The Sergeant snapped that it was a kind of bird.

Kirwan nodded but then was stuck again, 'How do you spell budgerigar?'

The Sergeant rolled his eyes to Heaven, 'Just write down bird...B U R D!'

1945: My First Arrest

18 May 1945 was the most incredible summer's day. It was also my fourth day on duty in the Dublin Metropolitan Division and my first day to go it alone without a mentor. I reported for duty at a quarter to two in the afternoon and was detailed to patrol Meath Street and the Coombe, all by myself. The Station Sergeant, a rugged Kerryman, with a heart of gold, was showing a flattering confidence in my abilities. Before I set out he told me that I wasn't to do anything foolish and was to refrain from getting involved in situations I couldn't handle by myself.

I was feeling good. Here I was, with not a care in the world, patrolling the busy city streets, enforcing law and order as I enjoyed the afternoon sunshine. I really liked the Coombe and Meath Street beat. There was plenty of activity and lots of people to bid the time of day to. As I passed Killeen's drapery shop, in Meath Street, I caught my reflection in the window and could hardly believe that the young man in the brand new policeman's uniform was my lowly self.

As I strolled past Saint Catherine's Church my new found confidence took a dive when Father Gleeson, the parish priest, came rushing out to me, 'Guard, there's one of them auld "sponkers" in the Church and she's roaring drunk. Go in and arrest her!'

I was both alarmed and confused. What in God's name was a "sponker"? And did I have the authority to arrest anyone in a church? Wasn't a church a place of sanctuary? I was almost sure I had read that somewhere. What if I arrested this woman, whoever she was, and it turned out that I hadn't the authority to do so, she could sue me for wrongful arrest and false imprisonment. I'd be ruined. More than likely I'd be thrown out of the force and my wonderful career would be in tatters, and all inside my very first week too. I was already picturing how my mother would once again have to hide me in the parlour, when I had returned home in disgrace!

Happily, my dilemma resolved itself when the lady in question emerged from the church and staggered dangerously down the steps, coming to an unsteady stop in front of me and the priest. She was small in stature with a slim build, about fifty years old, her complexion was a mixture of red to purple hues and her hair was grey, the same colour as her full-length coat that had seen better days. Perched on the side of her head was a big hat with a gigantic feather pointing skywards. And she was maggoty drunk.

As she was now standing drunk in a public place I felt my confidence return. This was it. I was on the threshold of making my first arrest and I was determined not to make a mess of it. I placed my hand on her shoulder and addressed her in my best authoritative voice, 'I am arresting you for being drunk in a public place and I am taking you to the station where you will be charged with the offence of drunkenness!'

I didn't expect any trouble. I was an officer of the law and assumed I would be treated as such. I took hold of her arm to lead her back to Kevin Street whereupon she roared, 'Take your filthy paws off me, you buttermilk bastard! Get back to the bog you came from. I've met your culchie lot before, you think you can come up here and walk over the likes of us when you don't know your arse from your elbow!' I was mortified and not just from her personal attack but also that she chose to do this in front of a man of the cloth. My cheeks were on fire.

When I had succeeded in regaining some composure I decided that firm action was called for as it was blindingly obvious that she was not going to come along peacefully. I asked her for her name and she reluctantly gave it to me, Julia Cornweight. I asked for her address and she replied, 'Number One, Open Air, Dublin City'. I should tell you now that a "sponker" is a former lady of the night, that is, one who has passed her sell-by date and is now reduced to living rough, sleeping in doorways or on the landings of tenement buildings. It is not a pleasant life and comes as no surprise that many of them turned to the comfort of alcohol. Julia, it later transpired, gave herself a lift fuelled by Red Biddy or Johnny Jump Up, made from a concoction of a half pint of methylated spirits and a bottle of the cheapest *eau de cologne*.

I took a firmer grip of her arm and said, 'Come with me, Madam. I'm taking you to the station'. We walked a couple of paces before I realised that she had somehow managed to get her left leg in front of me, interrupting my purposeful stride and tripping us both up. We fell out onto the street, with Julia landing on top of me. In just a few seconds a sizeable crowd of onlookers assembled to watch the show. They gave us a rousing cheer and burst into hearty applause. Julia had won the first round.

It was now a few minutes past three which meant that the crowd was suddenly extended to include the local children that had just come out of school. Traffic had come to a standstill and it really felt like the entire city was waiting for me to make my next move. Perhaps it was my close proximity to the church but I was suddenly inspired by the most wonderful idea. Amongst the audience was a Dublin Corporation street cleaner, complete with his handcart, shovel and brush. I told him, 'I am taking a loan of your handcart but, don't worry, I'll get it back to you as soon as possible'. He made no reply as I gently lifted Julia into the cart and closed the lid over her head. The fun truly started then. She kicked, she screamed and said curse words I had never heard the likes of before. Suffice to say that if cursing was Olympic sport, Julia would have won Gold!

I asked one of the schoolboys to push the cart to Kevin Street, for which I would give him sixpence. He was delighted to oblige, as were his mates who all clamoured for my attention. We set forth in procession. The boy pushing the cart, followed by his mates, followed by some of the onlookers, with me bringing up the rear doing my best to keep my distance from the screams, pretending as best as could that I had no part in the shenanigans.

Convinced that the Sergeant was going to think me some sort of police genius, I allowed myself to daydream about the possibilities of him recommending me for an appointment to the Detective Branch. All in all I was pretty chuffed with myself.

Outside the station I resumed charge of the handcart, paid my courier, and pushed it into the public office. The Sergeant did not greet me with open arms; instead, he let an earth-shaking roar at me, 'What in the name of Holy Jesus have you got in that cart?' Undeterred, I answered, 'A prisoner, Sir!' To prove this, I gently upended the card, allowing Julia to roll out onto the floor. The Sergeant was in no mood to be impressed, 'And why didn't you just bloody phone for a prison van?' I stared in confusion, 'What sort of van is that, Sergeant?' He spluttered, 'Good God Almighty! Didn't they teach you anything at all in the Depot?' I told him that I had honestly never heard of a prison van before but that I would know for the next time. He shook his head, 'Sonny, the way you behaved today makes me doubt that there will be a next time for you. Now, put the prisoner in the cell and get back to your beat, and never ever again transport a prisoner in this manner!'

Well, that was not the reaction I had been expecting. Surely he could have commended me even a little on my imagination and initiative.

That evening Julia was duly charged with drunkenness. I asked her if she wished to make a reply and she said, 'Well, if it's yer man Goose's Beak up on the perch, tomorrow, I'm a goner. He's nothing but an evil bastard!' I assumed she was referring to a member of the honourable judiciary but didn't ask her to elaborate.

The following morning I made my way to the Charge Court at the Bridewell for the hearing of the charge against my first prisoner. It was my first time inside a courthouse, I hardly knew what to expect. Prisoners that had been arrested the previous day had been collected that morning between half four and six o'clock from the various stations around the city. They had then been taken to the Bridewell where they were given breakfast and access to washing facilities. I reported to the Court Sergeant who informed me that my prisoner was in cell number fourteen.

She looked like a completely different person. She was clean, tidy and her hair was neatly combed into place. Her outfit which had appeared so outlandish and dishevelled yesterday now gave her a touch of class, topped off with that righteous feather that stood to attention over her head. After the roaring and the curses I did not expect the warm smile and greeting she gave me, 'Good morning, Guard, and how are you on this lovely day?' As I answered her I began to feel terribly sorry for her. How on earth had such a nice woman ended up in the state I had found her in yesterday? I began to comprehend the devastating effects of the methylated spirit and the *eau de cologne* cocktail.

'I suppose we'd best be moving over to the court, Guard. Do you know what Justice is sitting?' I hated telling her that I had no idea who was on today. I began to lead her out into the yard when she stopped me, 'Wait a minute. You're only a rookie so you probably don't know. All prisoners are supposed to be taken through the underground tunnel into the court to stop them from escaping'. She smiled at me kindly, 'But don't worry about that, Guard. I'm not able to run anywhere, with the way I'm feeling this morning'.

Down in the basement there were a number of other prisoners with their arresting garda escorts, all waiting to be called before the Judge. They presented a right miscellaneous collection, male and female, from the obvious "down and outs" to the well-dressed conmen and fraudsters.

Julia sat on the bottom stair, telling me, 'Find yourself a seat, Guard, and take the weight off your poor feet. We could be here a while'. I think she realised that I was starting to panic. I felt I could confide in her that it was my first time in court. She nodded, 'Ah, don't worry yourself. It will all be over in five minutes. Just make sure that you speak up when you're talking to the Justice. They act like they're God above and go mad when they can't hear a witness'.

After what felt like an eternity, a voice called, '54A (my district number) versus Julia Cornweight!' 'That's us!' said Julia, 'Good luck to you, Guard. Please don't be too hard on me'. We headed up the stairs, Julia leading the way. I was a bundle of nerves and had to admire her composure. When we reached the court room she discreetly pointed out the witness box for me while taking her place in the dock. She acknowledged the justice with a graceful bow of her head while he grunted, 'Not you again!' I studied the judge and concluded that Julia was right; he did look like a goose's beak.

The Court Clerk handed me the bible and I took the oath as loudly as I could without actually shouting. I began to present my case, 'Justice, between three and four o'clock yesterday afternoon I was on duty in Meath Street. Father Gleeson, the Parish Priest of Saint Catherine's Church, told me that…' 'Stop, Guard!' roared the Justice, 'I want evidence!' My goodness, surely there was no better evidence than the words of the parish priest. Perhaps the Justice was of another faith and had no respect for the Catholic clergy. 'Come on, Guard, come on! We don't have all day. Let me hear your evidence'.

My own nerves were choking me. I had no idea what he meant, no idea what I was supposed to be telling him. The silence clanged in my ears. A senior guard, realising I was absolutely stuck, came over and whispered in my ear, 'Tell the auld so and so what you actually saw, not what you were told by someone else'. I could have hugged the man and managed to get through my presentation without further interruption from the bench, skipping over Julia's bad language and name calling, while also omitting to mention the means of transport by which she had arrived at the station. It felt like the right thing to do.

When I finished the Justice asked Julia if she wanted to give evidence on her own behalf. She shook her head, 'No, Your Honour, just to say that it was a drop of Red Biddy I had taken and it went straight to my head. If you give me another chance I'll give it up altogether. Lately it hasn't been agreeing with me at all.' The Judge looked positively unmoved, 'Didn't I hear all this from you before?' Julia smiled, 'How right you are, Your Honour! Sure you have a great memory but I promise faithfully that if you could see it in your heart to giving me one more chance I will never trouble you again. God bless you!' Giving nothing away by his expression, the Justice asked, 'How many previous convictions does she have?' The Court Sergeant's answer was not good, 'One hundred and twelve, Your Honour, for loitering, prostitution, larceny, assault, malicious damage and drunkenness.' The Judge shrugged, 'Just as I thought. I am convicting the defendant of the charge and hereby sentence her to three months imprisonment.'

I was well and truly shocked. For some reason I had not thought about what would happen today, that when I arrested someone and brought them to court they could very well end up in jail. It was heart-breaking. Julia had no friends, no money, no home and was now going to jail for three long months because of me. In fact it was too much to bear. Without stopping to think I got to my feet and nervously asked the Justice if he could see his way towards being a bit more lenient with the defendant. To my astonishment he replied, 'Very well, Guard. I'll reduce the sentence to one month's imprisonment'.

Julia rose to join me, 'Well, God bless you, Your Honour, and you too, Guard!' We both left the courtroom and headed back downstairs where I deposited her back in her cell. As I turned to leave she reached out to shake my hand, 'Goodbye now, Guard, and thanks for everything. I'll see you in a month's time. And don't forget to report the result to your Station Sergeant. You don't want to be in trouble with him again'. I wished her well and left her, a lot wiser than when we first met. I learnt more from her about court procedure than I had in all the time I had spent in training in the Garda Depot.

The next day the evening paper, *The Mail*, carried a brief report of the case beneath the caption, "Lady with One Hundred and Thirteen Convictions!" It was noted that Garda 54A had charge of the case, my name wasn't mentioned. I didn't know whether to be thankful or sorry about that.

Julia was back in court six weeks later, charged once more with drunkenness and disorderly behaviour. I was glad not be involved with another arrest.

About two year later she fell down the stairs of a tenement house and died two days later in the Meath Hospital as a result of her injuries. I went to her funeral in Mount Jerome, a small affair consisting of eight people including the priest. I felt honour bound to go as a tribute to her for all that she had taught me, not just about court procedure but also about the

53

frailty of human nature and how important it is for a policeman to remember to look beyond the criminal to see the human being.

1945: Passing the Buck

It was a beautiful morning in May and I was strolling down the South Circular Road. I was working the early shift, from six o'clock to two in the afternoon, with a forty-five minute break at nine o'clock. I arrived at Dolphin's Barn just before eight o'clock where I was going to be inspected by the Duty Sergeant. My mood was light and relaxed, I felt confident that despite my few weeks of practical experience I would be well able to handle whatever came my way.

I saw the woman immediately and knew there was something very wrong. She was coming at me in what I can only describe as a fast trot, a woman in her fifties, dressed in a red woollen dressing gown and pink slippers. As soon as she saw me she let out a scream, 'Guard! Guard! There's a dead man in the canal, at the bottom of our garden'. With that my relaxed morning stroll was at an end. Good Lord! Had he been murdered? What on earth was I supposed to do? In short, I discovered I hadn't a clue.

What had I learned about homicide in the Depot? I must not have been paying much attention on the day on which we covered that topic. In any case I presumed this sort of thing was happily relegated to places like New York. However, I suddenly remembered a phrase I had heard, something about preserving the scene of the crime –but how was I to preserve a bit of the canal? Then it occurred to me that the woman might be wrong. Maybe the man wasn't dead; maybe he was just tired after a long swim. Well, anything was possible, wasn't it? At least now I knew what I had to do first, and that was to make sure I really did have a dead body on my hands.

As I accompanied the woman back to her house I had the presence of mind to ask practical questions, such as when she had first seen him and did she recognise him. In fairness, despite her agitation, she did her best to furnish me with as many details as she could while I did my best to write them into my notebook as we walked along at top speed. No, she didn't recognise him and she had seen him as soon as she opened her bedroom curtains about thirty minutes earlier.

I had time to think about the fact that if this did turn into an actual murder investigation then I, as the first Garda on the scene, would surely have my name and, with a bit of luck, my photograph in the newspaper. They would be so proud of me back home in Leitrim. I would be quite the celebrity on my next visit.

The woman lived in a terraced house on the South Circular Road. At the back of her house was a long, narrow garden that extended all the way back to the canal. I followed her through a side gate and admired her tidy garden with its flowerbeds bursting with colour. We made our way down a concrete path while I braced myself for God knows what. I saw him instantly and there was no doubting it, he was dead and floating in the water. Fully clothed, he was even wearing a tweed cap which remained perched on his head.

But how had he died? Was it suicide? Was he pushed? Was it accidental or was it actually a case of wilful murder? This last thought made the hairs stand up on the back of my neck. First things first, I quickly said a silent Act of Contrition and a few Hail Marys for the happy repose of his poor soul.

Now, what should I do? The woman watched me anxiously waiting for me to take charge. In no way did I want her to see my lack of confidence so I attempted to look as authoritative as possible, sagely nodding my head and telling her that she had no need to worry now that I was here. I realised I had to notify my superiors so I told her to wait right there, I remembered seeing a phone box outside the Church at Dolphin's Bar, so off I ran to put in a call to the station. I took off in the direction of the church but was happily waylaid when I bumped into my Duty Sergeant. In all the fuss I had completely forgotten he was coming out to meet me.

My relief was immense. I was heartily glad to be no longer in sole charge and was also keen to learn from him what to do in such a situation. He remained remarkably cool and showed no sign of panic or excitement. I guessed he must have been through something like this many times before.

His first question was an obvious one, 'Are you sure the man is dead?' I replied in such a way that he should know that that was the first thing to occur to me too. He nodded, 'Right, let's go take a look. Lead the way, son!'

The Grand Canal divided the "A" and "G" Garda districts of the Dublin Metropolitan Division. The "A" Division comprised of Kevin Street, Kilmainham and Newmarket Station while the "G" Division included the Sundrive Road, Crumlin and Terenure Stations.

On the way to the canal's edge, my Sergeant took a long pole that was propping up the woman's clothes line. I assumed that he thought he would need it to lever the body out of the water and assured him that the body was right beside the bank nearest to us. 'Yes', he said, 'I thought I might have a problem, alright'. Not fully understanding what he meant but not wanting to ask any potentially daft questions I led him down to the water.

When he saw the body he removed his cap and said a few prayers for the deceased. Then he leant over and placed the top of the pole under the man's right arm, giving it a good, firm push. The body moved across the water and gently came to rest on the southern side of the canal, that is, in the Sundrive Road Garda Sub-district. I watched in complete bewilderment but would not allow myself to ask any questions in case I displayed a blatant want of intelligence. Surely this was some part of police procedure that I had completely forgotten about.

The next thing the Sergeant did was put the pole back under the clothes line. I waited for enlightenment. Accordingly, he turned to me and said, 'Now, young man, I have an urgent task to perform. I have to inform them lazy bastards in Sundrive Road that they have a dead body in their Sub-district. It'll give them something to do to justify their wages.' I said nothing to this; in fact, I may have been genuinely speechless. He continued, 'I've a piece of advice for you so listen carefully. The less writing you have to do in this job, the less chance you have of getting yourself into trouble.' With that, he turned on heels and was gone.

I realised that I had just received my first lesson in how to pass the buck!

Ladies of the Night

I was on night-duty one July evening and had just arrived back at the station for my break at half past one in the morning. While I was there a gentleman who was well known to the guards came into reception seeking Garda assistance. His nickname was Crutch Kelly owing to an unfortunate accident that resulted in the loss of his leg, thus requiring him to get around on crutches. Crutch was married to Rosie Kinnane, a former "Lady of the Night", who, on marrying him, solemnly vowed to give up her past way of life in order to be a loyal and loving wife. It was a fortunate circumstance for her. At forty-five years of age she looked it and could not have expected the same level of business to have continued for much longer. Other women ended up on the streets when they reached a certain age and lost their ability to draw in customers.

Crutch worked every evening selling newspapers outside St Patrick's Cathedral in Patrick's Street. To supplement this meagre income he went out to Greenhills at night, to trap and snare rabbits and then sell them for a shilling. In those days once you crossed over the bridge at Dolphin's Barn it was all green fields with the exception of houses on Sundrive Road.

This particular night Crutch arrived home at one o' clock, four or five hours before he was expected, owing to a sick stomach. Home was a room on the fourth floor of a tenement house in Coombe Street, for which he paid two shillings and sixpence a week. You could imagine his displeasure at finding his wife back at her old job, in bed with a gentleman who on being surprised by the arrival of her husband, nevertheless refused to leave until he had gotten what he paid for. Crutch needed our help. The Sergeant detailed me to accompany Crutch back to his flat and remove the man.

Because I was only a recruit my Sergeant deemed it necessary to point out the law in such a situation, 'When you get there, have Crutch tell the man to leave. If he refuses to, you have the legal authority to forcibly remove him. And when you get him out on to the street break the knucklebone of the fornicator's arse with a good kick!' Certain that I could carry out the first part of the instruction, I was less confident that I could comply with the second.

With those clear instructions ringing in my ear Crutch and I walked back to Coombe Street. Thanks to the lights being out we had to climb the four flights of stairs, to the flat, in darkness. The room was a miserable one but probably a typical one for the time. It was a furnished flat, so there was some furniture: a bed, an old ragged sofa, a gas cooker, one small table and three chairs. The smell in the room was as bad as the building itself and there were bits of broken glass everywhere. I couldn't wait to get back outside but first I had a job to do and it wasn't an easy one. For one thing the "fornicator" was a docker, so he was big and burly. He still didn't want to leave, and the situation was further complicated by the fact that Rosie was holding onto him, she didn't want him to leave either and lose whatever sum of money had been agreed for their exchange. It took some effort but I finally succeeded in getting him out of the room and down the stairs, with the constant fear that we might fall and be seriously injured.

I thanked God when we both reached the street safely. My job was done, though I did refrain from fully complying with my Sergeant's instructions, I did not bother delivering that kick.

***

Prostitution was common enough on the streets of Dublin. I remember another July evening when I was patrolling Meath Street. My route took me past the three storey house of Mrs Conneberry who kept ladies of the night, by the night, as long as they could pay the toll of a shilling. If they couldn't pay up they were not allowed inside. As I was walking by, there was a young girl, about nineteen years of age, sitting on the step outside the house and she was crying hard. I stopped and asked her who she was and where she was from. It took a while because she was so upset but eventually she managed to tell me her story.

She was from Castlecomer, where her father held a responsible job in a local creamery. She had been attending a boarding school, only returning home for the holidays. One night, when her parents were asleep, she slipped out to go to a dance; it was her summer holidays after all. There she met a boy she liked and sometime later found herself pregnant. When her father heard the news he put her out of the house, telling her he never wanted to see her again. Not knowing what else to do she made her way to Dublin where she reluctantly found ready work on the streets. She had had the baby weeks earlier, given it up for adoption, and found it necessary to return to selling her body in order to survive.

She was sitting out on the steps this night because she hadn't a shilling to her name. I had untold pity for the poor girl so I gave her the required shilling so that she could have a warm bed at least for the next eight hours or so. In the meantime I took her father's name and address. As soon as I got back to the station I wrote to him, explaining what his daughter had been forced to do in order to earn money to survive. I told him that it wasn't too late to save her, if he'd only come and take her home. The letter was posted the very next morning and I received a swift reply, a very pleasant note thanking me for my interest but advising me that, 'as far as I am concerned, my daughter is dead". Unfortunately his reaction was very typical back then.

Mrs Conneberry in my opinion was a cruel, cold-hearted harridan. How could she leave a young girl outside at night-time, knowing that she had absolutely nowhere to go? Whenever she saw a garda she would coo, 'Oh, good evening, Garda, I'm delighted to see you around. I keep a nice class of girl here. In fact when the Tourist Board is busy they send me girls to keep'.

Who did she think she was fooling!

It is dangerous work and always has been. I was surprised at the variety of men who availed of the services of these women. Quite a lot of them were otherwise decent, upright citizens while others were downright dangerous. Assaults on the women were a frequent occurrence, either from their own customers or from other prostitutes. Of course there were also the pimps to be dealt with. These men were running profitable businesses around the entire Coombe area: Meath Street, Francis Street, Engine Alley and Swan Alley. The youngest girls I met were about eighteen years of age while some poor women were obliged to keep working into their fifties. If they stopped they would surely have starved. The guards knew them all. Life only got tougher the older the women got. Most of them ended up homeless, a few of them were forced to shelter on the landings of the tenement buildings, leaving them vulnerable to God knows what.

I never saw that girl again but I prayed that somehow her life much improved, leaving her free to walk away from such an awful occupation.

Meeting Nancy

On 1 July 1945 I was detailed by the Duty Sergeant to investigate a complaint from Laurence Roantree, of Congress Dairy in Marrowbone Lane, regarding youths breaking several of the windows in his dairy buildings. It was about half ten at night when I knocked on the front door which was opened by the most beautiful girl I had ever seen despite the rollers she was wearing in her hair! I announced that I was here to inspect the damage and she told me that her parents had gone to the pictures but she could tell me anything I needed to know. This was music to my ears.

She introduced herself as Nancy and brought me inside to show me the five windows that had been stoned. There is not much conversation to be made about broken windows. I asked about their financial worth but Nancy didn't know the cost so we agreed that she'd have her father ring me with the total. I thanked her for her time and left, with every intention to return as soon as I could.

About four nights later I knocked on the door again and, this time, I had to hide my disappointment when Nancy's mother answered the door. Introducing myself I asked if there had been any more damage. The answer was no and I could think of no other reason to remain on the doorstep. All I could do was wish her a good night and be on my way.

I allowed a few more nights to go by before I tried my luck again. This time I was rewarded when Nancy opened the door. There were no rollers in her hair and she looked even more beautiful. We discussed the break-in for as long as possible before I moved onto other subjects. Then, taking a deep breath, I told her that I had the following night off and wondered would she like to come to the pictures with me. She thought for a minute or two before saying yes. We agreed to meet outside St Catherine's Church on Thomas Street, where Robert Emmet, the Irish nationalist and Republican had been hanged by the British, although I can assure you that at that moment, such macabre historical thoughts were far from my mind! You can be sure that I skipped through the rest of my beat that night.

The following night, I was much relieved and delighted when the lovely Nancy arrived at St. Catherine's. We got the bus to O'Connell Street and went to see a film in the Carlton Cinema. Unfortunately I don't remember which film it was but I suppose the film wasn't important. What I do remember is that we got a double seat at the back of the cinema. These seats were extremely popular with young courting couples. However I never even put my arm around Nancy because I wanted her to know that I was a gentleman, in the hope that this wouldn't be our one and only date.

Afterwards we got the bus back to Thomas Street and stood outside her house talking for ages. Or maybe it would be more true to say that I did most of the talking not wanting the night to end. She was a great listener, although she did tell me about her job, the huge responsibility of looking after the accounts for her father's dairy. She explained about the big overheads in running such an operation, the feeding of the herd of Friesian cows, paying for the cows to be milked and then organising and paying for the deliveries. At one point she asked me if I liked milk. I was cheeky, 'Yes, I do, but I would prefer a kiss'. She laughed, 'Ah, but you are not getting one tonight!' This pleased me no end, 'That presupposes that there will be another night?' She laughed again, 'Well, that's entirely up to you'.

Of course there was a second night and a third. In fact we began to see one another two and three times a week. She had a quiet intelligence that set her apart from the other girls I had dated and she was definitely the best-looking girl I had ever gone out with. We went to dances, saw numerous films and took many a long walk up to Islandbridge. I brought her home to Leitrim to meet my family for a two week visit. They all took to Nancy immediately as did she to them. She laughed when she told me afterwards that before she travelled to Leitrim, she had been picturing my mother, who by then was a widow, (my father had passed away from stomach cancer in 1945), as a frail, little old lady. She got the land of her life when she was greeted by a large as life robust woman who almost squeezed her to death with the strength of the hug she gave her when she arrived!

From the moment I had met her, I had told my family all about my 'city girl'. It is true to say that they had some difficulty in coming to terms with the fact that, while she was from the Liberties, the heart of the city, her family ran a thriving dairy business with a herd of over one hundred cattle. However, as soon as they met Nancy, they knew that, far from having any airs and graces of urban sophistication, she was as down to earth as could be and had no issue with 'mucking-in' with how things were done in the country. As soon as she had arrived in Cloone, word went forth among the neighbours that Michael Bohan's 'intended' was now available for general inspection as such and a steady stream of visitors found reason to call by to meet the girl herself. Not only that, but Mother, obviously very proud of my choice, despatched us to go and visit any of those neighbours who hadn't yet had the pleasure of being introduced to Nancy. On one occasion, we were instructed to call to the nearby Carroll household. Paddy and his wife, Ellen were delighted to receive us and while they enquired about life in Dublin, I could see that they were simultaneously giving Nancy the 'once-over'.

Encouraged by Nancy's apparent interested questions about their farm and way of life, the couple suggested that she might like a little tour of the holding. Nancy agreed enthusiastically, while Ellen appeared to be somewhat surprised by her ready acceptance. 'Will you be alright in those nice shoes, Nancy?' 'You won't be too cold now in that light coat will you?' Ellen's concern for this lightweight city girl was apparent. With Nancy having assured her that she would be absolutely fine, we headed out to the farmyard.

We firstly proceeded to inspect a small brood of laying hens and while she was loud in her praise of them, I know that Nancy was silently thinking that they could hardly be compared to the many dozen to which she tended back home. We then progressed to a field at the rear of the property. On approach, the couple was flanking Nancy on either side explaining to her that they had something really special to show her but that she wasn't to be nervous.

When we reached our destination, they exclaimed, 'Well, Nancy, what do you think of those then? Pigs! Bet you've never seen those before and so close too. Now, don't worry, you're grand, they can't get near you, they're well fenced in.' Searching Nancy's face for the expected signs of being completely overawed by such a spectacle, not to mention some anticipated terror, they were obviously disappointed that she wasn't reacting as they hoped. As Nancy was obviously at a loss as to what to say, I stepped in to relieve her of having to break the news to Paddy and Ellen. 'Sure she has twice as many pigs at home in her own backyard. She feeds them every day and helps get them ready for market!' Poor Paddy and Ellen's faces were a picture. 'Pigs, in Dublin City, I never heard the like', exclaimed Paddy. 'Well you learn something new every day.'

Not wanting to offend, Nancy kindly assured them that by comparison to her family's pigs, the Carroll's animals had a very happy and healthy glow to them, something which was obviously the result of being reared in the good clean country air. Somewhat heartened by this, the couple suggested that perhaps a cup of tea and some soda bread would be in order at this point. The next event on their planned itinerary, a visit to see their herd of three Friesian cows, had, it seemed, been unexpectedly cancelled!

Nancy's two week stay in Cloone was such a success that when the time came to return to Dublin she shed many tears. She had fallen in love with rural life.

Six months after knocking on Nancy's front door I knew I wanted to marry her. I always looked forward to seeing her again and loved her company. She admitted that she had liked me from the first night we met and had even resolved to make sure to bump into me on my beat if I hadn't returned to her house.

We got engaged soon after but it would take a few years before we had saved enough money to marry.

To Drink or not to Drink

It was Christmas Eve, 1945, and I was sitting in the Reserve Room in the Garda station with my two great friends, Joe Holden and Mick Daly. We were detailed for work over the Christmas. In those days young, single guards were not eligible for any Christmas holidays. Joe and Mick were enjoying a few bottles of stout between them while I, a pioneer, stuck to a mug of tea.

With work finished for the day Joe and Mick decided to go to Wynn's Pub in Meath Street and invited me to join them which I did. They had more stout while I had a bottle of lemonade. At the second round the boys concluded that I needed to have a proper drink in honour of the festivities and a glass of port wine was ordered for me. I drank it once I got over the initial taste. I also drank the seven bottles of stout that were put in front of me, one by one, throughout the rest of the evening.

We left Wynn's and headed over to John Ryan's pub in Bonham Street where I had a small whiskey followed by four more bottles of stout. At this point it will probably be obvious that I had properly acquired a taste for the stuff. When the pub closed we reluctantly left and headed back home to the station. I was stumbling and giddy and my friends urged me to straighten up as we approached the door because, once inside, we had to walk by the Sergeant. I believe I wished him a very Happy Christmas though I don't remember doing it. In fact I don't remember anything much until I was called for mass on Christmas morning.

The day after St Stephen's Day I was on duty at the banks of the canal where the body of a woman had just been pulled out of the water. A barge had lifted its anchor and brought the body up with it. It was a woman who had gone missing on 22 November, the day a thick, heavy fog had encased the city. She had left her house, that evening, to visit her daughter, a route that took her along by the canal. The poor woman must have become confused and in her disorientation had missed her footing, plunging into the freezing water.

Her body was badly decomposed. A crowd quickly gathered as she was laid out on the banks for all to see. My Sergeant and I stood by, waiting for the ambulance to collect her. One of the onlookers asked, 'Is she dead, Sergeant?' The Sergeant did not bother to hide his impatience at the stupidity of the question, 'Well, I'm not a doctor but I don't think I'm letting out any State secrets when I tell you that she's been in the canal for over a month which would lead me to believe that it's more than likely that she is probably very dead indeed!'

I accompanied the body to St Stephen's Hospital, to certify the cause of death. After the paperwork was completed, the young doctor asked me if I would like a drink. Feeling like an old hand after my indulgence on Christmas Eve, I willingly accepted. He brought me down to a room in which there were three kegs of Guinness sitting side by side on one long table. The kegs had been sent over by Guinness's brewery, for the medical staff. (Now that I think about it, I don't recall the Gardaí ever receiving a similar gift from the company that was fervently supported by a lot of the staff in Kevin Street.) Both the floor and the table were covered with the remains of what must have been a great Christmas party. There was broken glass everywhere, along with crumpled up coloured paper decorations. Obviously, this was well in advance of the concept of 'health and safety' in the workplace.

The doctor apologised for the state of the room and also for the lack of glasses. All he could give me was an empty jam jar which he filled to the brim with stout. I assured him I had no problem with this. We pulled out a couple of chairs and sat there drinking for the rest of the evening. In all honesty I cannot recall a single subject that we discussed, only that it was a most enjoyable few hours. My shift ended but I never signed out. Meanwhile, back at the station, another friend of mine, Jim Hennelly, on hearing that I had accompanied the body to the hospital quickly put two and two together. Anticipating that my state of inebriation might cause me difficulty in returning to the station, he duly to escort me home. God only knows how many jam jars I had consumed by then.

Not surprisingly, I was in a wretched state the next morning. My forehead felt it was being gripped by some sort of clamp, while my throat and stomach seemed to be clamouring for my attention any time it wandered to my sore head. I went out for my patrol and quickly decided I needed a drink. I had heard from my more experienced colleagues that it was the best cure for a hangover.

There were plenty of pubs on my beat but I chose Bakers at the corner of Thomas Street. Inside there was just one customer. I recognised him; he was a dubious, shady individual with a police record. Ignoring him, I ordered a bottle of stout and sank into my seat, pleading with myself to feel better. My stout arrived and I began to work my way through it, although not without some difficulty. A few minutes later the barman brought me over a second bottle, telling me quietly, 'This is from your friend', as he nodded briefly in the direction of his only other customer. I sat there for a few minutes, allowing shame to wash over me, a sobering experience if ever there was one. What would my mother think of me? Here I was, a member of An Garda Síochána, and a former pioneer, drinking on duty and now having drink bought for me by an out-and-out criminal. It hit me quite forcibly that I was letting her down as well as myself and the job. I didn't acknowledge the man or the second bottle which I left untouched. I simply asked the barman what he was drinking and bought him one back. The next thing I did was walk out of the pub and make my way to the nearest church where I took the pledge again.

I didn't drink again for another 37 years.

1946: Lough Derg

Three fellow guards and I decided to go on pilgrimage to Lough Derg. It would be our first time to do this well known three day pilgrimage of prayer, fasting and sleep deprivation, on the island on a small lake in Donegal, known as St. Patrick's Purgatory. I booked a passage with the Legion of Mary and we got the train with them from Dublin. When the train pulled into Balbriggan one of the women in charge came into our carriage and said, 'I've heard that there are four guards on this pilgrimage and I want them to distribute water to the pilgrims'. We kept our heads down, unwilling to be pulled into having responsibilities on our weekend off from work. She left only to return five minutes later and point at us, 'You, you, you and you! I know you are guards by the look of you. Come with me!' It never occurred to us to refuse. Reluctantly, we got up and followed her.

The train left us at Enniskillen where we were getting on a bus for the remainder of the journey. It was spilling out of the heavens and very windy. The bus brought us to the small jetty where we would be taking a rowing boat across to the island. First we had to pay the nun who manned the little office on the mainland. We handed over ten shillings for three nights' bed and board, along with two shillings and sixpence for the rowing boat.

I had done some research before we arrived and had read about a rowing boat that sank in 1894 and all the pilgrims on board were drowned. One of the victims was a red-haired priest and legend had it that a second boat would also go down, which too, would have a red-haired priest on board. Just to be sure, I scrutinised my fellow pilgrims but could see no red-haired priests amongst them so felt relatively safe on the choppy water.

On arriving at the island we had to remove our shoes and socks and immediately commence saying aloud the Rosary. Walking in one's bare feet was difficult thanks to the small, sharp pebbles that had blown in from the lakeside.

After that we had to do what were known as the six beds. These were small structures with a nine inch high wall on the outer ridge. We walked around each bed, saying six Our Fathers, Hail Marys and Glories. Next we had to kneel at the cross in the centre of the bed and recite the same amount of prayers again before we completed the first of the six beds. This was followed by more prayers as we knelt at the water's edge and then we went into the church for more of the same again. It amounted to about an hour of praying.

Having finished our first station we were allowed to go for our first meal which consisted of as much tea and coffee as you liked, with dry bread or toast. That was the sum total of the menu on offer. We spent that first night praying in the church, not having any sleep whatsoever. At seven o'clock, the following morning, the priest arrived to say mass in Irish. There was an extremely long sermon and most of us were nodding off to sleep, not only from having stayed awake all of the previous night but also from the sheer boredom. Out came an elderly woman with an umbrella who moved through the rows of pilgrims, freely poking anyone in the ribs that looked to be asleep, scolding them in a fierce whisper, 'Wake up, you're on a pilgrimage!'

Beside the main basilica, there was a sort of mess room, one for the women and one for the men, with a turf fire that never gave out as much heat as one would have liked. Set upon the fire was a ten gallon metal pot with a tap at the bottom of it from which you helped yourself to the famous Lough Derg 'soup'. You could have as much as you liked which was something since it was far from filling, consisting solely of hot water, salt and pepper. I must say, however, in its defence it was great for warming the stomach.

A heated discussion commenced in the men's mess room about the six beds, about which one was the most difficult one to do. The general consensus was that St Brigid's bed was by far the toughest. One of the contributors to the debate was an American who made us gasp with his solution, 'Listen here to me, you guys! A tonne of cement would fix this goddamned joint and I'd be happy to pay for it!' I gathered it was his first and likely, his only visit to Lough Derg!

Sunday was a rest day and it was a beautiful one, the sun shone down making everyone feel less of a martyr. There was a young couple from Longford sitting at the lake's edge. They were sharing a rug which was covering their legs against the lake breeze. The Monsignor in charge glanced over at them, said nothing and went back into the parochial house. He emerged again a few minutes later, having ordered a rowing boat from the mainland. Marching over to the couple, who were not doing anything untoward, I assure you, he loudly addressed them in front of the rest of us, 'Be off with the pair of you! You are going home!' The girl burst into tears while the boy looked utterly horrified.

I was outraged. There had been nothing indecent about their behaviour and now they were being sent home, having to tell their parents that they had been evicted from Lough Derg, of all places. I imagined they would have some difficulty explaining that they had not been guilty of any wrong-doing. Before they left I approached them and explained that I was a guard from Kevin Street Station in Dublin. I gave them my name and the phone number of the station and told them that if they had any trouble with their parents, they were to have them ring me and I would assure them that they had done nothing wrong. I never heard from them afterwards I assume that they had been able to convince their parents of their innocence. Either that or they never actually told about their ignominious departure.

Many years later I brought Nancy to the island. She vowed never to return and never did.

1947: Kevin Street Garda Station's Christmas Party

Some weeks before Christmas 1947, a few of us were sitting around the fire prior to going out on night duty at ten o'clock. Joe Holden, my good friend, commented on how Christmas was going to be a lonesome affair in the station for those of us who were rostered for duty. Everything closed for the holidays, the dance halls, the picture houses and the pubs.

We mused on his words for a minute or two before I had a sudden brainwave, 'What if we hold our own party here on Christmas night? We could invite our girlfriends and friends'. Even as I was talking the idea was taking firm root in my head. 'We wouldn't have to supply much food since everyone would have had their big dinner. So, all we would need is tea, a few sandwiches and some cake.' I looked at the others for their reactions.

Tom Mullarkey piped up, 'Surely you wouldn't hold a party in this mess room?' He had a point.

The mess room was far from decorative and comfortable, not the type of room you would invite a girl to spend an evening in.

'No', I agreed, 'But we could hold it in the band-room'.

The room had been built specifically for the Dublin Metropolitan Police's (DMP) band. I assumed it was big inside. None of us had ever seen the inside owing to the fact that it remained under lock and key for the last thirty years or so. I assumed, however, that if it was purpose built to

69

accommodate a band, then surely it had to be of a good size.

Tom asked an obvious question, 'But do you think the Super would give us permission to have the room?'

Shrugging my shoulders I replied, 'I won't be able to answer you that until I have a word with him tomorrow.' Stage one of my plan was to be undertaken first thing the following morning.

Pat McCormack, our Superintendent, was a product of the old DMP and an absolute gentleman to his fingertips. The following morning I went to his office and outlined our plan for Christmas night, asking if we could borrow the band room for our party. As usual his attitude was one of generosity and support, 'Go ahead. It sounds like great fun. In fact I think I'll come along myself with Maura my daughter '. With that, he reached into his pocket and gave me five pounds towards the expenses. When I asked about the key of the room he told me to get it from our Staff Sergeant Neary, who was in charge of stores. I thanked the Super for his help and sped out to find the Sergeant, who had a slightly less helpful attitude to the matter. Indeed, on being asked for the key, his reply was, 'No! That room is not to be opened'. I was incredulous, 'But I have the Super's permission!' He was not impressed, 'You might have his permission but I have the key, and you're not getting your hands on it'. There was nothing for it but to go back to the Super who immediately instructed the Sergeant to hand over the key to me. You can imagine the Sergeant did this very reluctantly while I did my best not to appear smug.

If a thing is to be done, it should be done as well as possible. To that end my friends and I formed a party committee. I was Chairman, Tom was Secretary and Dan Friel was Treasurer. There was no shortage of members. Now that I had the key we could go and inspect our premises for Christmas night. A group of us went to view it together. I turned the key in the lock and pushed over the door. What a sight greeted us. If you have ever seen the old black and white film, 'Great Expectations', you will sympathise. The film sprang to mind as I peered into the vast darkness. Remember now that the room had not been opened in thirty years and my God but it looked it. The room was dark despite the big windows, thanks to the thick dust and several layers of spiders' webs. The floor was thickly carpeted in dust while the pervading smell was decidedly musty, to say the least. However, there was no denying its space; it was a perfect place to hold a party. We congratulated ourselves and commenced upon our first important work, as a committee, that is, vigorously scrubbing, dusting and polishing in that order.

After several days of Trojan work, the room finally looked the part. We needed to organise the music. Billy Driver, a Church of Ireland man, was a commercial traveller for Rowan Seeds and a frequent visitor to the station. He had a great liking for the guards and would call in for a cup of tea and a chat. As it happens he was also a brilliant pianist. When he heard about the party he told me that if we got him a piano he would be delighted to play for us on Christmas night. I was thus commissioned to approach the music shop, Walton's, in Camden Street. They were famous for their Saturday programme, "If You Can Sing A Song, Do Sing An Irish Song". I passed the shop regularly on my beat and, as a result, knew Mr Walton pretty well. I asked him if we could hire out a piano from him for the night and he said no, 'But you are very welcome to have a loan of one, if you can provide the transport'. We shook hands, 'That won't be a problem!', I assured him.

Tommy O'Neil (known as Civie O'Neill) was an ex-British army soldier who visited the station every evening at seven o'clock after the domestic staff went home. He took it upon himself to attend to such chores as washing dishes and running errands for the guards. His speciality was bringing something like a suit to the pawn shop and getting the best price possible for the guard in question. Maybe he missed the military life. He lived alone and the station was his only social outlet. We all contributed a few shillings for his help – he wasn't short of money – and he was perfectly happy with that. When he heard about the party he acquired a hand-cart and we brought a piano down from Walton's.

The rest of the music would be supplied by Garda Jeff Durkan, who played the flute and Garda Peter Hegarty on the accordion.

Once news went abroad about the party, there was huge interest, especially when members in the other districts heard about it. So many wanted to come that we had to start turning people down as there just wasn't the room for the demand. As the numbers continued to increase I realised we didn't have nearly enough cups, saucers and plates to serve the tea. I knew a Mrs Walsh who lived in Carmel's Hall, just off Francis Street. She provided the catering at race meetings and other functions, so I asked her for a loan of a hundred cups, saucers, spoons and plates. 'Certainly, Guard, as long as you have them back to me, washed and dried, by six o'clock on Stephen's morning as I need them for a race meeting'. I willingly agreed.

The local publicans were hugely generous too, sending in bottles of Guinness and beer, three bottles of whiskey and a few bottles of wine, which wasn't as popular then as it is now. Of course only the men would be drinking alcohol, and only enough to get merry, while the girls would, by choice, be sticking with the cups of tea. As we weren't selling the drink we didn't need a license to dispense it.

At eight o'clock on Christmas night we opened the newly polished doors to the band-room and were met by a sizeable crowd. The place was hopping within minutes. It was a huge success, with the music and dancing not stopping until half past seven the following morning! We served the tea and sandwiches at midnight and washed the dishes immediately after, delivering them to Mrs Walsh's house at five o'clock, an hour before her deadline. I wanted to be sure to show our gratitude for her co-operation.

Everyone told us that they had had the best of fun and thanked us for our efforts. Indeed we received such a positive reaction that it inspired us to think bigger. What if we could hold dances every Sunday night to which we would charge a nominal entrance fee? This would allow us to raise funds to spice up the Recreation Room which was quite bare apart from a few uncomfortable chairs, one small table and the fire place. There were no books, no magazines and no radio. Plans were soon afoot to buy a billiard table, some easy chairs and a writing desk. We decided that these weekly parties could be held in the gymnasium which was attached to the station.

Having acquired permission to use the gym, previously the training centre for the DMP, we set about taking care of the domestic details. It was a very large room with a timber floor that sported a lot of black knots that would create difficulties when it came to dancing. First thing first, we bought an electric plane for forty-five pounds and did a right good job, levelling out the floor. Next we built a stage and thirdly we decided to give ourselves a name. From now on we would be known as the Kevin Street Garda Recreation Club. We printed up membership cards, with the Garda crest and the name of the member. You didn't have to be a Guard to join, otherwise we couldn't meet girls, which for many fellows was the primary aim of the exercise! Regarding interested parties, however we were very select. For instance, anyone with a criminal record would have their application rejected.

Music would be supplied for free by musically talented members of An Garda Síochána who called themselves The Castle Arcadians. The first of the Sunday night dances proved to be even more successful than our Christmas party and the recreation room was reborn and completely made over thanks to the profits generated.

About a year after we started the club I applied for a transfer. I was hoping to get a station close to home in Leitrim. Nancy and I were engaged by now but accommodation in Dublin was scarce and far too expensive for my wage packet. Nancy suggested that if I got transferred to a rural station we could afford to get married and start our new life together. In the end I was granted a transfer to Fernanes, in the division of West Cork.

Just before I left Kevin Street the Deputy Commissioner, WRE Murphy, called a meeting. He had quite a record before joining the guards. He joined the British Army at the outbreak of World War 1, in 1914, and went on to become the youngest ever to be appointed Major General. He had a Master's Degree in Education and had been a School Inspector before joining An Garda Síochána. News about our recreation club had spread throughout the force and the Deputy Commissioner called a meeting to discuss it on 2 April, inviting two delegates from each district of the Dublin division.

At the outset he explained he had no objection to what we were doing

73

in Kevin Street and proved this by congratulating myself and Dan Friel on our achievement. However, he said that if the club was to continue he wanted it done on a divisional basis, meaning that the profits should be distributed beyond our station. I pointed out that it would be most unlikely that we would receive any assistance, (maintaining the premises, organising the food), from members in outlying stations such as Blackrock, Finglas, Whitehall and so forth. This would mean that money would be handed over to them while they made absolutely no contribution to the dances. Mr Murphy accepted that as a consequence but held fast, 'It has to be on a divisional basis and that's my final word'.

Moving on he asked if there was anything else that needed to be discussed. I spoke up again deciding to seize the moment and mention something that continually frustrated me. 'Yes, Sir! My district number in Kevin Street is 54A which is displayed here on my uniform and is the only form of address made to me by my superiors. I don't have a name. Sir, my parents paid good christening money to have me called Michael Francis Bohan and they would be shocked to know that their son is now being referred to by a number, like a criminal out on license'. The Deputy Commissioner nodded his head, 'You have a point, Guard. I assure you that that practice will stop hence forth'.

Sure enough, the next morning each station in the Dublin Metropolitan Division received a memo from Mr Murphy detailing that members were now to be referred to by rank or Christian name. The practice of using numbers became a thing of the past, something I am particularly proud of. I was congratulated and thanked by other guards. Naturally some of our superiors struggled with the new directive. A good friend of mine, Pat Clarke, whose number was 57A, was on duty in Francis Street, being inspected by 17A, Sergeant Tompkins. The Sergeant's greeting was now out of fashion, 'How are things on your beat, 57A?' Guard Pat responded in kind, 'Everything is fine. Thank you, 17A!' I think the Sergeant got the message.

The Recreation Club continued to be a huge success. After I left, Detective Inspector Ned Garvey, later Commissioner, known for his organisational skills, was invited to take over the running of the club. Under his leadership the club went from strength to strength until, two years later, there was enough money to buy a house in Harrington Street. He had it gutted and converted into the Garda Club where Bingo became one of the more popular forms of entertainment. Later on he had enough money to buy the adjoining house, knocking down the walls and enlarging the club premises. After that, with the Recreation Club profits, land was bought at Stackallan, at the foot of the Dublin Mountains, on which was built a golf course. A couple of years later a second golf course was built at Westmanstown.

As far as I am aware, An Garda Síochána is the only police force in Europe, if not further afield, to own two golf courses, perhaps in some way thanks to the 1947 Christmas party we held in Kevin Street.

Night Patrol

It was January 1947 and it was cold, very cold, the middle of one of the coldest winters ever recorded in Ireland and subsequently known as 'Black 47'. Six inches of snow covered the paths which made my nightly patrols not a little unpleasant. Guards weren't supplied gloves back then so I could only keep my hands firmly in my pockets as I walked the empty streets.

The night patrol would have been a lonely few hours except for the fact that I had a stray dog to keep me company. I named him "Nights". He waited for me outside the station at ten o'clock and would walk with me until six o'clock the following morning. At the beginning of my month he was a skinny thing in need of food but he was well fattened up by the end of the month because I would bring him into the station, for my break, where he would be given his share of whatever was going. With fifty-eight single men living in Kevin Street's depot he was never short of a bite to eat.

One particularly cold night, Nights and I were patrolling Meath Street when Sergeant Meehan, my duty sergeant, came out of Engine Ally and made a curt welcome, 'Take your hands out of your pocket, 54!' By way of an obvious explanation I offered, 'But, Sir, it's an awful cold night'. He was unmoved, 'It doesn't matter. It looks bad in the eyes of the public'. The only people around were the two of us and of course, the dog. I gestured at Nights and asked, 'Would you construe "His Nibs" as a member of the public?' Sergeant flared up, 'Less of that smart talk or I'll report you for insubordination!'

I felt like saying, No you won't, Sergeant, because you wouldn't be able to spell the word. What I actually said was nothing as I took my hands out of my pockets. Oh, how I cannot abide people who abuse the little bit of authority they hold, just for the sake of it!

I will never forget the snow of that year, it lasted for weeks. The first falls arrived at the end of December 1946 and continued well into the month of March. It was accompanied by a chilling wind and the kind of gripping cold that sinks itself into your bones and refuses to leave. Having come in from night duty at six am one morning, I took off my overcoat and it was actually frozen solid, so much so that I was able to put it standing upright on the floor ! In later years, if ever any of my children complained about the cold, I would tell them that however cold they thought it was, it was nothing like 'Black 47'. On hearing this, they would always reply, 'yes we know, the year that the overcoat stood up on its own!' I don't think they actually believed me.

One night I was patrolling Meath Street. I came to the junction at Engine Ally and saw what appeared to be a bundle of old clothes behind a lamp post. Going in for a closer look I realised it was a homeless man, in his sixties, and he was dying. I knelt down and lifted him up onto my lap. There was no response. I said an Act of Contrition into his ear. He gave a low moan and passed away in my arms. I rang for an ambulance who took him to the Meath hospital where he was pronounced dead on arrival.

His name was John Byrne, of no fixed abode, a former British Army soldier who fought in the First World War. I attended his funeral in Glasnevin Cemetery which was pitifully small. There was just the priest, two undertakers and myself. I thought about that poor man for months afterwards. It was such an awful way to die, all alone in the cold.

He wasn't the only person to be killed by the weather. There were plenty of homeless in Dublin and nowhere for them to go. They could get a penny dinner at the Adam and Eve Church or else there was the sanctuary of Father Leeson who provided dinners at his church in Meath Street. He ran an advertisement on the front page of the *Irish Independent*, in the top right-hand corner, which read: "Charity covereth a multitude of sins. Please give generously to the Penny Dinners in Meath Street".

When the guards came across a homeless person on a night patrol, they would bring them down to the South Dublin Union (later Saint James Hospital). The porter answered the door and the guard asked him to look after the individual who was given a bed for the night along with breakfast the following morning. It was huge building that performed many functions. I recall a census being taken in 1947, to estimate how many ration books were needed, and it was found that there were two thousand residents in the South Dublin Union.

1948: President Seán T O'Kelly

Seán T O'Kelly was the second president of Ireland, serving office from 1945 to 1959, and a popular one by all accounts. There are many amusing anecdotes about his time as President, but these two are probably my particular favourites:

The President and his (second) wife, Phyllis, were attending the Dublin Spring Show in the Royal Dublin Society (RDS) Ballsbridge, Dublin 4. They made a great arrival in a state carriage that was drawn by no less than four horses. As soon as the Presidential couple entered the arena the army band struck up a rousing Presidential Salute that unexpectedly also struck terror into the hearts of the four horses. Taking fright they set off again at a magnificent gallop around the arena, with our President holding on for dear life to his good wife who was of a much more solid build than her husband.

In those days the Gardaí wore a cape which was rolled up and thrown over the shoulder as long as the weather was dry. A very brave Garda ran out in front of the horses and flung his cape over the heads of the first two bringing them to a prompt stop. As you might imagine he won a huge round of applause from the excited crowd. The Presidential couple was unscathed from their close call although I don't believe that they put their fate in the 'hands' of the same team of horses any time soon!

***

In those days it was customary for an tUachtarán na hÉireann (President of Ireland) to throw in the ball at the start of an All-Ireland football or hurling final. The procedure began with the President of the GAA (Gaelic Athletic Association) taking to the stand and inviting President O'Kelly to throw in the ball. Now, the President was a small man. As he was walking out onto the pitch in front of a cheering crowd, one bold Dubliner, sitting in the Cusack Stand, let out a roar: 'Would someone ever cut the f***king grass so we can see our President!'

1948: The Beginning and Ending of a Riot

Back then unemployment was high while wages were low. I'm sure a lot of people today would say that nothing has much changed since. One evening a big protest march had been organised, the climax of which was to end at the front of the Dáil. People wanted the government to do something to improve the situation. The crowd gathered at about ten pm and things began to grow heated between the marchers and the guards whose job it was to keep the event under control. Unfortunately that was proving to be a difficult task after several of the marchers took to throwing stones and sticks at the guards. Things turned quite ugly with the guards finding themselves under pressure and extremely vulnerable.

Sergeant O'Rourke, originally from the West of Ireland, advised his Superintendent, 'You'll have to organise a baton charge, Sir. Four of my men have been injured'. The Superintendent, who did not want a full scale battle on his hands, replied, 'No. Hold on until I pray to the Holy Spirit and ask Him for guidance'. O'Rourke was far from impressed. 'F**k that!' were his exact words. Next he went and stood behind the wall of Gardaí that separated the marchers from the government buildings and shouted, as loudly as he could, 'Guards, draw your batons!' He paused for a couple of seconds and then roared, 'Charge!' I never saw a disturbance end so quickly. The street literally cleared in a matter of minutes with no further bloodshed. Meanwhile, no further instruction had been issued from either the Superintendent or the Holy Spirit!

1948: Homeless Couple, Dublin

There was a cycling rotation shift for night duty in Kevin Street. One perk of being on the cycle shift was that we received one pound for the use of our bicycle. The other perk was that it meant we were free to roam the district which made it difficult for our Sergeant and Inspector to keep an eye on us. However, we were obliged to return to the station once every hour in case the Sergeant had a problem he needed help with. For many people today, I'm sure it's difficult to imagine such basic policing methods, well before the days of radios, let alone mobile phones. At that time there were only two patrol cars for the division and we shared one of them with the B District, the area around and including College Street and Harcourt Terrace.

I returned to the station, as instructed, at midnight and the Sergeant told me that there was a homeless couple sitting on the path in Francis Street. The woman had called Dublin Fire Brigade three times to have her companion taken to hospital by ambulance but each time he flatly refused to go so the fire brigade had no option but to ring us. The Sergeant told me, 'Go and sort it out but whatever you do, don't bring them back here. I don't want prisoners tonight'.

When I got to Francis Street I found that I knew the couple very well. Emily Grace O'Donnell and Patrick Fitzgerald: both of no fixed abode. Patrick had been a member of the British Army during the 1914–18 war. He didn't look very well and told me that he had been in Leopardstown Hospital the previous month. During his absence Emily, his common–law wife, had embarked on a relationship with another gentleman. This, he felt, was her reason for calling the fire brigade, to get rid of him and leave her free to meet her lover.

There were quite a few homeless people living on the streets back then and the guards would never leave them sleeping on the street. Leo Enright had a local business in Engine Ally. He kept jarvey cars and horses in a stable there that was always dry with plenty of straw and this is where we would take the homeless souls we came upon during night patrols, checking up on them throughout the rest of our shift. There they could enjoy a good night's sleep in peace in relative safety.

While I was chatting to Patrick, Jim Hennelly arrived on the scene and I asked him to go to Enright's yard and fetch a handcart. The couple were elderly and a little worse for wear so I didn't want them walking to Engine Ally. Jim arrived back with three other guards but, instead of a hand-cart they were pulling a jarvey car behind them. Normally this was the job for a horse and Leo did great business driving tourists around the capital.

Between the four of us we got the couple up on to the front of the carriage. Then we pulled it together up Francis Street, on to Thomas Street and down Vicar Street until we finally reached the stable. It was after one in the morning by then and we settled the couple in the hay. I checked on them three times before my shift ended at six o'clock and they were sleeping soundly.

Many years later, when I was a sergeant in Kilbrittain, West Cork, I had an opportunity to give a night's accommodation to a missionary priest, Father Eddie Roche, an Augustinian friar, who was returning home from Africa for a holiday. When missionary priests arrived back from somewhere like Africa they would overnight in John's Lane Seminary, in Dublin, to give them a chance to acclimatise themselves to the Irish climate. Prior to Father Eddie's arrival, his mother had a stroke and naturally his home was in some disarray. Fr. Eddie had spent his first three nights in John's Lane but thereafter had nowhere to stay for the remainder of his sojourn back home.

Meanwhile, two weeks beforehand, Nancy and our two children had left for Dublin, due to an outbreak of polio throughout West Cork, leaving me with two spare bedrooms. On hearing of Father Eddie's plight, I told his brother Maurice, a friend of mine, that he was welcome to stay with me as long as he liked. My offer was gratefully accepted.

So, Father Eddie came to stay. He proved to be great company, although this was unfortunate in one sense as we sat up late into the small hours, talking, exchanging stories about his missionary work in Africa for my stories about patrolling the streets of Dublin. Father Eddie told me about a night he had spent in Dublin a few years ago. He had returned from Africa and was spending the required first night in John's Lane. Finding it hard to sleep, he got out of bed and was looking out his window which faced onto Thomas Street. To his surprise he found himself, as far as he was concerned, witnessing a great act of Christian charity. He saw a number of guards pulling behind them a jarvey car in which was seated a grey-haired couple and came to the conclusion that their horse had died in transit and the guards had elected to pull the couple home, 'I was so impressed with this act of Christian charity that I said a rosary for the guards'. My face was beaming as I said, 'Well, thank you, Father. As it happens I was one of the beneficiaries of that rosary' and told him the real story. We had a great laugh about it.

My parents John and Bridget Kate on their wedding day, Easter Monday 1919.

Cloone Boys' National school, Second Class 1934.
I am pictured in the back row, first on the left.

My darling wife Nancy, 1944

GARDA SIOCHANA RECREATION CLUB.
KEVIN STREET

★

The Committee requests the pleasure
of the company of

Miss Nancy Rowntree

at their
Social to be held in Kevin Street
Recreation Hall.

On *17th March '48* Commencing at *9 p.m.*

John Lee,
Hon. Pres.

Nancy's invitation to a Garda 'Social' in Kevin Street,
St. Patrick's Day, 1948

Our Wedding Day, 15th October 1951

Presenting the winner's trophy to 'Miss Crookstown' Fernanes 1952

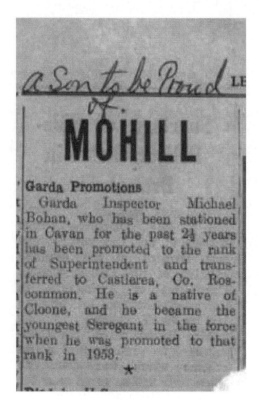

A Son to be Proud of.

MOHILL

Garda Promotions

Garda Inspector Michael Bohan, who has been stationed in Cavan for the past 2½ years has been promoted to the rank of Superintendent and transferred to Castlerea, Co. Roscommon. He is a native of Cloone, and he became the youngest Sergeant in the force when he was promoted to that rank in 1953.

✳

A cutting from an article in The Leitrim Observer about my promotion to the rank of Superintendent, 1964.

It was posted to me by my mother with her hand-written comment on top –

'A Son to be Proud of.'

The proud father, myself with
John, our eldest, Kilbrittain 1953.

Anne and John, Kilbrittain 1957

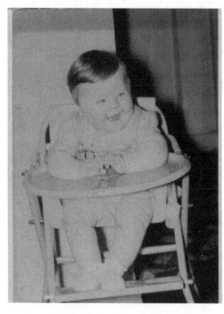

My beautiful son Michael, Cavan 1964.

The family in Drogheda 1966.
Back Left to right: Gretta, Nancy, Anne, John.
Front: Breeda in the pram and Michael on my knee.

Myself and Nancy at a Garda Christmas Dinner Dance, Butlins 1967

Michael on his First Communion Day 1971

With Dan Fakha, Mali, attending the 1981 Interpol Conference in Nice, France.

Greeting King Juan Carlos of Spain on his visit to Monasterboice, Co Louth, July 1986.

*Myself and Michael, June 2013 on the inaugural day of his reign as
'Festival King' at St. John of Gods, Drumcar. Co Louth.*

1949: The Synagogue, Dublin

One Sunday afternoon I was detailed for duty at a wedding that was taking place at the Jewish Synagogue on the South Circular Road. The Synagogue required the presence of the Garda Síochána for their weddings largely due to undesirables from the surrounding area who would attend the event in order to throw stones at the participants. I was standing outside and thus far, there had been no unwelcome guests. I started thinking about the ceremony itself. I had never seen a Jewish wedding and my curiosity got the better of me so I decided to go inside to see how it differed from a Catholic one.

Inside I saw the Rabbi, in his cap and vestments, standing behind a table, sheltered beneath a canopy. The next person who caught my eye was the bride, a beautiful young girl who looked to be no more than nineteen or twenty years of age. Her dress was breath-taking while her bare arms were weighed down with jewellery. I was shocked at the sight of her groom. At a guess he was in his late fifties, was bald and grossly over-weight. I supposed it must have been a match made by her parents. She was smiling brightly but I felt real pity for her, having to marry such an unattractive man who was old enough to be her father.

Towards the end of the ceremony the Rabbi poured wine into a glass and passed it to both bride and groom, who each took a small sip. The Rabbi took a sip too and then poured the remainder of the contents onto the ground, followed by the glass. He walked on it, breaking it into smithereens. Lastly the bride and groom, now husband and wife, walked on the glass fragments. I could only think that it might be some form of pledge against the consummation of intoxicating liquor. When the ceremony was over the guests and bridal party adjourned to the function room next door. To my surprise the groom invited me to join them for the meal which I was delighted to do. I cannot remember exactly what I ate, but there were lots of courses and all of them were delicious. Later on I even got to dance with the bride. All in all I thoroughly enjoyed myself but little did I know it was going to cost me.

The following week I went to confession, in those days guards went to confession once a month in Whitefriar Street Church, and it is fair to say that I didn't have a lot to confess for this particular visit. However, I did have a niggling doubt about my attendance, as a Catholic, at the Jewish wedding so, to keep my conscience clear, I decided that it was best to tell the priest and be done with it. I liked the priest; he was in his fifties, and always very pleasant to me. Nevertheless he almost had a heart attack when I told him I had stepped into the synagogue and then stayed to enjoy the party. Sounding genuinely horrified, he asked, 'Do you realise the grievous mortal sin you have committed?' I replied, 'As a matter of fact, Father, I didn't think it was a sin. I went out of idle curiosity and I have to say that it hasn't weakened my faith in the Catholic Church'. I could not believe my ears when he told me that he had no power to give me absolution because the sin was so serious, (apparently it was known as a "Reserved Sin"), and therefore only a bishop could help me out.

This was not good news. The archbishop, at that time, was actually the famous Archbishop Charles John McQuaid and I certainly did not relish having to request a meeting with him to seek his absolution. I had never met the gentleman but his reputation did not paint him as a warm or welcoming man, in fact quite the opposite. My only alternative was to stand up for myself right here in the confession box. With the little knowledge I had of Canon Law, learned from my school catechism and the Bible, I began my defence, 'Father, when I was studying for my confirmation I learned that a mortal sin has three important components: grave matter, full consent and full knowledge. Now, Father, I agree with you that it is a grave matter, and, yes, I fully consented to going into the synagogue but the third component is not probable because I did not know I was committing a mortal sin.

As I told you, I am a member of An Garda Síochána and if I arrest a person and charge him with larceny of property I must prove all the essential ingredients which constitute the crime of felony:

1.   That property was stolen

2.   That it had a value

3.   That, at the time of taking it, the accused had the

intent to deprive the owner, permanently thereof

4.   That the property had an owner

If I fail to prove each and every one of these, the accused is entitled, by law, to a dismissal of charges. Therefore, Father, comparing Criminal to Canon Law, I think I am entitled to absolution on the grounds that I did not have full knowledge in the committing of a mortal sin.'

Fortunately for me the good Father saw my point. He gave me absolution there and then along with the stern warning that I was never to step inside another church that was not Catholic. I accepted the absolution on his terms and resolved to cease at once, my curiosity about the practices and ceremonies of faiths other than my own!

1940s: Favourite Stories

There was a garda stationed at Buncrana in Donegal who was an alcoholic and had been disciplined on many occasions for being drunk on duty and for neglect of duty. His most recent breach of the rules resulted in an order that he be transferred to Allihies in West Cork, the nearest Irish parish to America. The station was remote and was under the command of a very stern Sergeant who might straighten him out for once and for all. That was the first part of his punishment. The second part was that he had to pay for his travel and transfer out of his own pocket. He was also fined five pounds.

On hearing about this decision he applied for ten days special leave. His application was returned by the Superintendent and he was told to state the purpose of his request. The Garda pointed out that he had been ordered to transfer to Allihies at his own expense and since he had no bicycle he had estimated that it would take him ten days to walk from Buncrana to his new station. His application was given sympathetic consideration and the upshot was that he was now allowed to make the journey on public transport at public expense.

On his first day he reported to his new Sergeant who was known for being tight fisted. The Sergeant gave his new charge ten summonses to serve which meant a significant amount of walking in order to deliver each one by hand to the various recipients. The nearest address was four miles from the station while the farthest one was twelve miles away.

The Garda set out and many hours later stopped to ask a farmer, who was cutting his hedge, for directions to the next recipient, 'How many miles is it to Michael Lynch's of Mylane house?'

'Whisha, Garda, I'd say as the crow flies it would be a good six miles from this spot'. The Garda who was understandably tired and in no mood for ambiguities snapped, 'Well, if the f***king crow was walking, how many miles would it be?'

***

There was a Garda who was stationed at Farnaught Station in County Leitrim. One day he was detailed for two shifts, the first one lasting from ten o'clock in the morning until two o'clock in the afternoon and the second one from nine o'clock to midnight. When he arrived back to the station at two o'clock he was in time to receive his wages from his Sergeant. With the money safely ensconced in his pocket he took himself off to have a pleasant lunch at his local pub, where he indulged himself reasonably well in the intake of intoxicating liquor.

When he reported for his second shift that night, the Sergeant realised that he had been drinking but he judged that he hadn't taken enough alcohol to charge him with being drunk on duty. Nevertheless he deemed it necessary to accompany the Garda on his beat, despite the fact it was a miserable night outside. He told the Garda, 'You'd best bring your walking stick; Joe Fleming has a very wicked dog!' In those days the guards carried a black walking stick with a silver mounting; it was part of the official issue. The Garda replied, 'No need for the walking stick, Sergeant. Joe Fleming is a decent man; he wouldn't leave his dog out on a night like this'.

They left the station and headed out into the rain, walking side by side in silence. However, there was an eruption forming in the Garda's belly. Owing to the number of pints consumed, a certain amount of gas was begging for release and, with no option but to comply with the demands of

94

his bloated innards, he gave in to a natural urge and there was a sizeable explosion from his rear. Neither man made a comment, they merely continued on with the beat. But that was not the end of it.

In due course the Garda found himself charged with a breach of discipline. The report read thus:

....in that you did, in the presence of your Sergeant, discharge foul air with more force and violence than was reasonably necessary.

He was fined two shillings for his foul conduct!

I found that file when I was working at HQ and was amazed at the wording of it. I thought it very well framed indeed. The kernel of the offence was that the foul air was discharged with more force and violence that was *reasonably* necessary. Had he gently eased out that foul air instead I doubt if the evidence would have been sufficient to sustain the charge!

1951: Marrying Nancy and Settling into Farnanes

In 1950, even though I was more than happy working in Dublin, I decided to apply for a transfer to a rural station, hoping that I might be sent to one in Leitrim. Nancy and I wanted to get married but needed to live somewhere cheaper than Dublin. A few weeks later I got my transfer, not to Leitrim but to Farnanes in County Cork. I had enjoyed my years in Kevin Street and was genuinely sad to be leaving friends and colleagues behind but, naturally, I was excited about the move and about starting a brand new life with Nancy. I left Dublin on 4 May 1950, starting work the very next day in Farnanes Garda station. Until we married, I would be living in the station itself. The next year we both saved hard and, as the wedding approached, I found us a house to rent.

One October afternoon I received a phone call from a distressed man who told me that he had called to see a neighbour who unexpectedly answered the door with a weapon, threatening to hurt anyone who came near him. The caller also told me that the man had a history of mental illness. He lived by himself in a house in Farran so I jumped on my bike and cycled the four miles to his place as fast as I could. When I got there I found a number of men standing outside the front door, along with William Carney, a senior guard, who informed me that the man was armed with a slash hook. Garda Carney had no ambition to step inside the house to disarm the assailant, and told me as much, therefore it was up to me to take action.

Now, I was rather mindful of the fact that I was due to get married the following week and most certainly did not want to greet my bride with my face and hands covered in cuts and bruises. Hoping that by now the gentleman had calmed down, I tentatively pushed open the front door and looked in. He was standing by the fireplace. As soon as he saw me he brandished the hook in my direction, screaming that he would cut my head off if I came any nearer. There was a wild look in his eyes and I didn't doubt him for a minute.

I took a few seconds to consider my options which were not as varied as I would have liked. Finally I hit upon an idea. Looking around the area outside the house I spied a large stone and picked it up. Returning to the front door, I did my best to remain hidden and flung the stone with all my might into the fire, causing a burst of angry sparks to fly out of the grate. As I had hoped, he jumped and turned towards the fire to see what had happened, giving me a brief opportunity to make a run for him. I pounced and managed to grab the hook from his hands. Once I had removed his weapon he was easy to cuff as he quietened down immediately, all the fight gone from him. When I brought him outside the crowd gave me a rousing cheer, presumably to express their approval that both myself and my prisoner were both alive and uninjured.

I had an ambulance come to his house and take him to a hospital in Cork City where he stayed for the next few months. It turned out he hadn't been looking after himself properly nor taking his prescribed medication. On his return to his house I called to visit him, keeping an eye on him at the same time. He was always most apologetic for his previous outburst. I felt very sorry for him as once I got to know him, he turned out to be a quiet and gentle character.

I married Nancy a week later, on 15 October 1951, in St Catherine's Church on Dublin's Meath Street. The wedding was typically early in those days; it was a ten o'clock mass, said by Father Bernard, the local curate. My brother Peter was the best-man while Nancy's sister, Detta, was bridesmaid. The ceremony was followed by a fry-up breakfast in the Clarence Hotel. There was a great crowd in the church, a mix of both families and my Garda colleagues. My relatives made the journey from Leitrim and stayed in the Ormond Hotel. I wasn't at all nervous but then I've never been the nervous type!

Outside the church, the stall holders stood to clap and cheer. They all knew me well as I had built up a good relationship with them over the years and had always done my best to treat them with respect and kindness. They had such a tough life, setting up in the small hours of the morning and plying their trade right through to the evening, six long days a week. I had great respect for them and often somehow managed to 'overlook' serving them with summonses, if they hadn't got the required license from Dublin Corporation.

One of my favourites was Mary Ellen Winters who sold fish from her stall between the junction of Meath Street and Thomas Street in every kind of weather. Every morning, at eleven o'clock, her husband would come by with her lunch of a bottle of tea and two slices of buttered bread. She had proved fearless one day when I arrested a very drunk and disorderly man whose friends gathered around me to rescue him. Mary Ellen got between them and me armed with her fish knife, shouting, 'First one to lay a hand on 54A, I'll let out his guts!' That blessed lady and her knife escorted me and my prisoner all the way back to the station.

Nancy and I honeymooned in the West of Ireland, spending a week in the Galway Bay Hotel and then returned to Dublin for one night before heading off for our new home in Fernanes. The house I had managed to rent for us must have been an early challenge for Nancy in our life together. In its hay day it was an RIC station and was very bare indeed. Nevertheless, rent was fair at ten shillings a week. Neilis Murphy, our landlord, had been a talented hurler.

There was no running water, no indoor toilet and not one electric light. To think I had brought a city girl who came from a house with all the 'mod cons' of the day, to live in a place like this! But she didn't baulk, even with the prospect of a daily walk up a hill to a stream which provided us with the water to cook and wash our clothes. It was a large two-storey house, with two rooms upstairs and a kitchen/dining room downstairs that we decorated ourselves. Before the wedding I had bought some furniture: a bed, dining room suite, lino for the kitchen floor and carpet for the stairs and bedroom. One advantage was that our bedroom was always warm thanks to its location over the kitchen which was well heated by the range. One problem was that there was a huge number of insects of various kinds, necessitating my having to spread a special powder all over the floor to try to orchestrate their elimination, a battle which continued for many weeks until eventually I got the upper hand.

The outdoor toilet was a 'special' one. It basically comprised of a bucket in the garden beneath a sheet of corrugated iron. It had once been housed in a small hut but over the years, the two sides and the timber door had fairly rotted away so our landlord put up three large sacks as a substitute, allowing us three separate entrances and plenty of ventilation. Oh my poor Nancy!

We shared the semi-detached building with another couple, Rita and Paddy Murphy and their adopted daughter. They lived in what used to be the Sergeant's Quarters which consisted of one bedroom upstairs with a dining/sitting room and a pantry downstairs. Rita was a retired nurse while Paddy was an electrician who left bright and early for work every morning, waking me up in the process. They always struck me as a very united couple. Every morning, without fail, Paddy would close the door behind him and shout up to his bedroom window, 'Goodbye, Rita! I love you, pet!' One morning I couldn't resist the temptation to reply to him, shouting, 'Goodbye, Paddy! I love you too!'

We finally got wired up twelve months later when the house was connected to the electricity supply. Nancy was in Heaven as we bought basic luxuries like an iron, toaster, radio and a proper cooker. What a difference it made to her life, especially when our first child, John was born

6 August 1952.

My work was quite different in a rural station from what it had been in the city. We did station orderly duty from nine o'clock in the morning until nine o'clock the following morning. There was relief for an hour at one in the afternoon and then we took our evening meal between six and seven o'clock. The long shift meant spending the night in the station. We worked three sets of eight hour shifts and two of twelve hours, with three days off a month – although, on the third day, you were obliged to relieve the station orderly for his lunch and then perform a four hour patrol. There was plenty of overtime to be sure but unfortunately there was no overtime pay to accompany it. After Kevin Street I found the station to be a very quiet one. The phone rang maybe one or twice every twenty-four hours. At ten o'clock every night we received a test phone call from the post office to make sure the line was working. I thought it a terrible waste of time.

The duties undertaken by the Guards in rural stations were many and varied and I suppose in many respects, really didn't come within the definition of real 'policing'. We collected agricultural statistics, we undertook compiling the census of the population, delivered pensions books and even recorded the daily rainfall. I especially enjoyed delivering the pension books to first-timers. There was always a great welcome, a completely different reception from when you delivered a summons to someone's door.

At one point seventy-five pension books were sitting in the station waiting to be delivered to various residents throughout the district. My Sergeant asked, 'Who is going to start delivering these? Do you think the pensioners are going to come by and get them themselves?' I badly wanted a day off to work in the garden so I asked him for a deal, 'How many days will you give me to deliver all of them?' He offered me two days to do nothing else but deliver the books; I was determined, however, to do it all in one day leaving a whole day for myself and my gardening duties.

The next morning I left the house at seven o'clock and spent the next seventeen hours on my bike with hardly a break delivering those seventy-five books, making it home ten minutes before midnight. The day after that

I thoroughly enjoyed planting the garden with carrots, onions, runner beans, lettuce and cabbage.

It wasn't unusual for us to forget to record the rainfall for two or three days. When we did, we would ring the nearest station to us, get their reading and come up with something similar.

There was a Sergeant in another station by the name of George Watson, a very precise and humourless man who never ever admitted to being in the wrong. He was not your average Sergeant in that somehow he owned a car and also a horse box when the rest of us thought ourselves lucky to have a bicycle. One time he forgot to record the rainfall for a few days and rectified it, as he saw best, by sending off the total amount of rain that was on the gauge on that particular day, claiming that it amounted to one day's worth.

His report was sent off to the Department of Industry and Commerce and there came back a swift reply telling him he must have made a mistake, and asking him if he would be good enough to check it again as adjoining areas had recorded no rainfall on that date. He wasn't. True to form he wrote back to confirm that he had made no mistake. A second letter arrived back telling him that he obviously had indeed made a mistake, that there was no way all that water was from one day's rainfall. He wrote back denying the charge. A third letter arrived but this time it was from the Assistant Secretary of the department informing him that he had made a mistake and if he didn't fix it there would be action taken. At this point most people would have simply sent back a new rainfall report but not this man. He took out his pen and wrote the following note to the Assistant Secretary:

'I reiterate what I have already said. I found 22 fluid ounces of liquid in the gauge on the day in question. Since you did not provide me with any scientific equipment to analyse the contents of the liquid I cannot state with any degree of accuracy whether I found rain or dog piss.'

Amazingly, there were no further letters on the subject.

***

I wasn't long in Fernanes when a farmer came in one evening asking for the Sergeant. 'I'm afraid he's out on patrol', I said, 'Can I help you?'

He explained that he ran a small poultry station where he kept pure bred Rhode Island hens and two of them were missing. He suspected his neighbour of stealing them. I took down all the details and assured the man that I would tell the Sergeant when he got back and we would come and visit him at his house.

I had no intention of telling the Sergeant just yet as I felt pretty confident that I could handle this case by myself. The first thing I did was get myself a search warrant and then I went out see the neighbour. I told him in no uncertain terms that two hens had been robbed and he was the prime suspect. He brought me around to show me his own hens. There were two red ones that stuck out very obviously from the rest of the brood. I also found a bag nearby containing lot of long red feathers. At this stage there was nothing else to do except to fetch the owner who identified the hens as his. However, I wanted further proof to be sure. By now it was dark so I picked up the hens and dropped them some distance from their alleged owner's house. We were both gratified as the hens took off towards his house without a moment's hesitation. To me this was ample evidence that the hens belonged to the first farmer.

His neighbour was charged and got the benefit of the Probation Act while I was delighted to receive a bonus of two pounds for good police work which I received just before Christmas.

1951: Fernanes: My First Appearance in a Rural Court

It was June 1951 and I was patrolling the main Cork, Macroom, Killarney Road, which was a busy one because it was the main artery between Kerry and West Cork. I stopped Mr Tom O'Shea, a Killarney man, in his hackney cab. It was a large car and he had six passengers with him. However, on checking his insurance, I found that he was only covered to carry four passengers so I duly prosecuted him.

The case came up for hearing about three weeks later in Coachford

Court, before District Justice Keely. There were few prosecutions apart from an unlicensed dog and a cyclist who had no lights on his bike. My case was the last one of the day. I stood up and gave my evidence. When I finished a gentleman got to his feet. He was the defendant's solicitor and began his cross-examination thus: 'So, you are the new Black and Tan in Fernanes?' I did not answer him. He barked, 'Are you deaf, Guard, should I repeat the question? Are you the new Black and Tan in Fernanes?'

Now, I wasn't alone. My Sergeant was in the court room sitting beside the Superintendent from Macroom who I had expected to be on his feet defending me from such an unfair attack. I looked over at him and he was just staring at the floor, obviously not planning to get involved.

Turning to the Justice, I said, 'Justice, I am not deaf. Thank God I have all my faculties but I must object in the strongest terms to these offensive remarks. I am not a Black and Tan, I am a member of An Garda Síochána, our national force, and proud to be so. Furthermore, my father and his brothers fought for Irish independence.'

The Justice shrugged, 'Ah, it was said in the heat of the moment.'

I could not believe my ears, saying, 'With respect, Justice, he repeated it.'

Somewhat reluctantly, the Justice said, 'Well, I suppose it was a bit harsh.'

The solicitor smiled, 'Don't worry, Justice, I'll rephrase the question. Are you the new terrorist in Fernane's?'

'That is equally hurtful and unnecessary, Justice', I protested, 'Please direct him to withdraw it'.

I was still waiting for the Superintendent to say something in my defence, but he never did. In my view, any Superintendent prosecuting in a District Court is under a moral obligation to protect their witness from an unfair attack be they a guard or a civilian.

The Justice addressed my superior, 'Superintendent, I cannot follow this case!' It now appeared that my evidence and the entire case were in question.

Now the Superintendent would have to get involved. And he did but, instead of coming to my assistance, he poured salt into my wound by saying, 'Justice, I'm sorry but the guard doesn't know what he's talking about.'

Incensed by this I declared, 'Superintendent, if you would hand me your guide (law) book, I'll convince this court that the submissions I have made are well founded!' I went on to read aloud from Section 57 of the Road Traffic Act 1933 which clearly laid out what an approved insurance policy was. Next, I produced a copy of Mr O'Shea's insurance which revealed that it did not meet the standard requirements. I handed everything over to the Justice who, after a quick perusal, saw the light, 'Ah, yes, I get the point, now.' It is a good thing that he could not read my mind or he would have heard himself being described as a complete idiot.

Mr O'Shea was fined ten shillings and the case was finally closed.

I left the court house and saw the Superintendent in conversation with my Sergeant. Never one to miss an opportunity I went up to him and tipped him on the shoulder, 'I just wanted to thank you, Sir, for your help and support.' Flicking a wrist at me, he said, 'Ah, these cases are too involved for the likes of you.'

'No, Sir', I replied, 'Not too involved for me but, perhaps, for you, the solicitor and the District Justice!' I walked away before he could say another word.

Later on, my Sergeant told me that when I walked off the Superintendent advised him, 'You'd want to watch out for that fella. He's a cheeky pup and will cause you no end of trouble.'

May I just add that, years later, on 6 June 1964, when that particular Superintendent retired, it was this cheeky pup that took his place!

1951: Electric Fence

I was still new to the area when a local farmer came into the station, one Monday night, to report that someone had stolen the battery that fired his electric fence. I told my Sergeant and we headed out to make enquiries. The battery had cost just over six pounds, a lot of money in those days. I was grateful for the Sergeant's company since I didn't know too many people in the area while I don't think there was a person in the locality with whom he wasn't on first name terms. We called in on another farmer in the area and told him about the fence. He shrugged, 'I hadn't heard anything about it, Sergeant, but come back to me on Wednesday and I'll see what I can dig up.'

The following day, Tuesday, my Sergeant was on a day off. At about two o'clock a car pulled up outside. The driver, a tall man in uniform, whom I guessed to be Inspector John Butler, got out. The Inspector was standing in for our Superintendent who was away on leave. When he strode into the station I stood up and saluted him. He didn't smile. Instead, he asked, 'Are you the buck from the city?' I bristled, 'With respect, Sir, part of that question is correct and the other part, I resent.' He ignored my complaint and asked another abrupt question, 'Is the crime solved?' Shaking my head I told him that hopefully it would all be resolved within the next twenty-four hours.

Obviously bored with talking to a mere guard he asked where the Sergeant was. 'He's on recreation, Sir.' In fact he had gone to a funeral. The Inspector's' eyes widened in mock disbelief, 'On recreation when there is a crime to be solved?' I was never one for keeping my mouth shut if I felt someone was being unfair, 'I don't know about that, Sir. But let me ask you, if the crime could not be solved for seven years, would that mean that the Sergeant would have to forego his recreation for as many years?' Staring at me as if he couldn't believe his ears, he bellowed 'Huh! I was right the first time, you are a buck!'

The next day was Wednesday and the Sergeant's friend was as good as his word. He was able to tell us who stole the battery and where it was. It turned out that the nineteen year old son of another farmer had taken it for his own fence. Since it was his first offence he got off with a stern warning. A good example of how a positive relationship with the locals is as valuable a police resource as the most sophisticated technology !

1952: Money Talks!

T.P. Howard was a popular local businessman whose factory, Howards One Way Flour, provided substantial employment for the surrounding area. He was also a Peace Commissioner and a gentleman in every sense of the word. It was with great sadness that we heard of his unexpected passing one Friday evening. He had been chairman of the committee that oversaw the parish dancehall. It so happened that the following Sunday the local hurling club were hosting a carnival in the hall, to raise much needed funds for the club.

Some people felt it would be wrong to proceed with the carnival two days after Mr Howard's death while others felt it should go ahead, as the club had booked it ages beforehand and already paid out for it so a cancellation would mean a loss of money. Quite quickly it became a hot topic and the town was divided over what to do.

Mrs Kane, a local shop-owner, rang the station and asked to speak to me. She told me about the trouble that was brewing and begged me to do something. I agreed to do what I could, 'Mrs Kane you have two cars at your disposal and I'll have a lot of visits to make. Can you make a car available for me at two o'clock?'

The first person I visited was Mrs Howard. I explained the whole situation to her, saying, 'If I know your husband he would allow the carnival to go head, and I'll make sure a mass is said for him.' Mrs Howard immediately agreed. After that I visited the others on the committee, some were harder to convince than others but eventually they all said yes to the carnival taking place. The last person, however, proved the most difficult of all. Father O'Driscoll was adamant that the carnival be cancelled and would not listen to reason. He wouldn't budge even after I told him that the widow and the other committee members were in agreement about the carnival going ahead as planned. Eventually I used my last resort, 'Father, I have heard that a novena mass is to be offered for Mr Howard. You are going to be asked to do it and will be paid twenty pounds.' The priest took a couple of minutes to decide that yes, perhaps the carnival could go ahead after all. Money talks!

1952: 'I think I'm a traveller, Sergeant'

My Sergeant was a very upright, overly conscientious man, particularly when it came to the policing of the local pubs. For instance, if he heard a publican was selling drink after hours you might have thought, from his reaction that the most atrocious murder had been committed.

And so it came to pass, on a beautiful June night, he heard a rumour about Sweeney's establishment, which was located at Rooves Bridge on the banks of the River Lee. It was a difficult place to get to. You had to push your bicycle up a hill for about four miles but then you could free wheel downhill for the rest of the journey. The Sergeant commandeered me to accompany him for the inspection.

Closing time during the summer months was half past ten. We arrived at the pub just before midnight and, sure enough, could hear the laughter and talk inside, confirming the Sergeant's worst nightmare. I was instructed to go around the back to prevent any escapes while he rapped authoritatively on the front door. As we both expected there was a rush to the back of the building but I managed to hold them in situ.

All told, there were twenty-nine people on the premises. The Sergeant and I began taking their names and also asking each individual why they were still in the pub. The most common excuse given was that they were out in the fields making hay, so they had only reached Sweeney's after ten o'clock. Sergeant's temper was as hot as the evening. He rounded on one fellow, asking him what he was doing on the premises. Affronted, the farmer replied rather sulkily, 'I came in for a bit of tobacco. Is that a crime?' Sergeant huffed and puffed, 'No, it isn't a crime. Did I say it was bloody crime?' The farmer shrugged his shoulders, 'No, but you'd swear it was a hanging offence with the fuss you're making.'

The Sergeant moved swiftly along to Connie Wilson who was living with Joe O'Keefe and his family, in Aglish, working on their farm. The Sergeant asked him for his excuse. Connie said, 'I think I'm a traveller, Sergeant.' He was told that he was wrong. 'But I think I am', persisted Connie, as politely as he could.

Just to explain; under the liquor licencing laws at the time, while the normal closing time in the summer was half past ten, any person who had travelled a distance of three or more miles was allowed to drink on the licenced premises until midnight, Monday to Sunday inclusive. Consequently, if any of the drinkers on the premises could prove themselves to have travelled three miles or more to avail of a drop of the hard stuff, then they were legally entitled to be on the premises until midnight. This was the reason why Connie had referred to himself as a "traveller".

The Sergeant didn't argue any further with Connie at that point but when we left the pub he said to me, 'The cheek of that fella, trying to pull the wool over my eyes!' I attempted to be diplomatic, 'Ah, forget it, Sergeant. Sure we have twenty-eight names. Just give Connie a caution.'

'No, I bloody won't!' was all I got.

The following day a guard from Bandon station drove up in the patrol car, marched into the station and dropped a large, heavy chain on the floor. 'What's that?' I asked. 'It's a chain, Sonny.' I bristled, 'Yes, I know that. Let me rephrase the question. What is it for?' The guard looked bored, 'I don't know. I was just told to bring it in and in my book a gentleman does what he's told.'

When the Sergeant came in he filled in the Duty Sheet, or roster. To my surprise I was down for a shift starting at half past four the following morning. It seemed that he and I were going to check on Connie's statement about whether or not he was a traveller by physically measuring the distance from the O'Keefe's house to the pub.

We all lived in the station; I was in the single quarters while the

Sergeant lived next door in the married quarters. He called me at four o'clock and gave me a proper breakfast. To be sure, the man had a heart of gold.

A half hour later we were on our bicycles. When we reached the pub, the Sergeant began to measure the distance using the chain, length by length, while we continued on foot, pushing our bikes. The chain was twenty-five yards long. He walked in front of me and dropped a stone for every twenty-five yards. As we reached O'Leary's Cross, which was a mile from the pub, we sat down and had a smoke, enjoying the early morning sunshine. When we were finished we picked up our bikes again and continued on with our task. When we were within a chain's link from the O'Keefe house, the Sergeant turned to me expectantly and asked, 'well is Connie a traveller or not?' I looked at him blankly, 'I don't know, Sir. I wasn't counting.' He scrunched up his face in surprise, 'Weren't you?' 'No', I replied, 'I wasn't.' So we had to cycle back to O'Leary's Cross and start over again. I asked why we couldn't just measure from the house back to the Cross but the Sergeant wouldn't hear of it, 'No, I won't do that. I have to measure to the property itself in case I ever had to give evidence on oath.'

This time when we reached O'Keefe's house we knew the exact distance and as it turned out, Connie was indeed a traveller by two lengths. Just as we reached this conclusion, Mr O'Keefe and Connie came into the yard, on their way to milking the cows. 'I'd say he's a traveller alright Sergeant' was Mr O'Keefe's only comment. The Sergeant was annoyed, 'Yes, yes. Alright he is!' He was in a foul mood now and refused Mrs O'Keefe's offer of breakfast, much to my dismay, as I was pretty hungry by then and assumed he was too. Fortunately he reconsidered his refusal and eventually changed his mind and we both went inside to a huge and delicious breakfast which improved his mood considerably for the ride home.

I knew that he quite fancied himself as a cyclist and he made sure that he started out ahead of me. I was cheeky enough to pass him by, pushing myself to get back to the station as fast as I could. When I got there I propped my bike up against the door, wanting to give the impression that I had been back ages when he arrived all red-faced and sweaty. All innocence, I asked in a concerned voice, 'What happened, Sergeant? Did you get a puncture?'

His reply was unprintable!

My Little Bonzo

Pat Guckian was one of my colleagues. A native of East Cork, he joined An Garda Síochána in 1923, two years before I was born. He was married to Vera and they had no children. He was also reputed to have plenty of money, thanks largely to a legacy left by Vera's wealthy spinster aunt. Despite his wealth, Pat was "extremely careful" with his cash. I once heard someone say that Pat could peel an orange in his pocket.

Pat and Vera had a Jack Russell terrier called Bonzo on whom they both doted. Every Sunday you would see the whole 'family' in their Morris 8 car out for their afternoon drive. Vera was behind the wheel, Pat in the passenger seat while Bonzo took full command of the back seat.

In accordance with the Finance Act of 1925, any person who keeps a dog aged one month and upwards must hold a license for them. Licences were easily obtained from the Post Office and cost a mere five shillings. Since the license expired on December 31 of the year of issue, it was in the owner's best economic interest to purchase one as early as possible in the New Year. One might imagine that the license was a priority for Pat, who loved his dog dearly and was, after all, a member of An Garda Síochána. However, one would be mistaken. Pat believed that the five shilling license was a waste of money and in any case who would be brave enough to prosecute him for such a trivial misdemeanour?

January came and went, as did February, March, April and May and still Bonzo had no license, a fact easily established since each week a copy of all licenses issued by the Post Office was sent to the local Garda station. Our Station Sergeant felt duty bound to bring the matter to Pat's attention, thinking that Pat had merely overlooked the task of buying a licence. He reminded him once and once again, and yet again, before realising that it was a deliberate decision on Pat's part, to avoid parting with five shillings.

Pat's answer was always the same, 'Don't you be worrying about Bonzo, Sergeant, he'll be licensed in due course.' But he never was.

Ironically, Pat was extremely dutiful and diligent in the enforcement of the Finance Act. In fact I would go so far as to say it was a sort of "pet" project for him, and he held numerous prosecutions against citizens of his Sub-district for their unlicensed dogs. As the months passed, the matter of the unlicensed Bonzo became more unbearable for the Sergeant. On the eve of his departure for his annual leave in July he issued a final warning to Pat, 'If you don't have a license for that dog by the time I come back I promise that I will personally prosecute you and, furthermore, I will initiate disciplinary proceedings that will cost a damn sight more than the five bloody shillings!' He slammed the door hard after him.

Much as I tried to pretend that I hadn't heard the Sergeant's threats, Pat felt obliged to pour oil on troubled waters and sighed heavily in my direction, 'Isn't it a little thing that upsets the man? Not to worry, he's all talk and no action. I know his form.'

In the Sergeant's absence, Pat, by virtue of his seniority – certainly not his ability – was acting Sergeant in Charge. A plan was slowly forming in my mind and when I went out on patrol I decided to put it into action. On finding a public phone box I rang the station. The phone was answered by Pat and I put on my best upper class accent, saying, 'My name is Kennedy and I'm an Assistant Secretary in the Department of Justice. I wish to make a serious complaint. Please put me on to the Sergeant.' 'Well now, Sir', said Pat, 'The Sergeant is on his holidays but I'm Acting Sergeant so I'll take down your complaint if you would just like to give me the details'. I took a deep breath, 'Very well, then. My wife and I are touring West Cork with Donal, our son. As a keen amateur photographer I stopped to take a picture at a very picturesque spot. A man told me it was called Rooskeymona.' Here, Pat interrupted me, 'Actually, Sir, I think you mean Rooskeynamona and you're absolutely right, it is a very picturesque spot. In fact it's where I live.'

'Well', I said, 'Whatever the place is called I was taking photographs when a black and white Jack Russell terrier came tearing out of a house and made a ferocious attack on my son.' I paused for effect before continuing, 'I am ringing you from Doctor Dolan's surgery. My son needed twelve stitches to his leg. As you can imagine, we are cutting short our holiday and returning home. Sergeant, I want this matter thoroughly investigated and I also want it on record that it is my considered opinion that the dog should be destroyed immediately because he is obviously a danger to the public!'

I could sense Pat's panic on the other end of the line but, to give him his due, he managed to maintain his professional manner, 'Yes, Sir, that sounds bad alright. Would you mind describing the dog again for me and also the house he came from?' I complied, first describing Bonzo and then Pat's house. Pat obviously decided it would be futile to pretend he had nothing to do with either of them, 'Well, do you know something, Mr Kennedy, that sounds very like my house that you've just described and, as it happens, I own a small black and white Jack Russell but – I promise you, Sir – he is a very quiet animal and wouldn't harm a fly.'

Raising my voice, I let fly, 'Are you calling me a liar, Sergeant? I have no doubt that that was the dog that attacked my son. Right, this is what we're going to do. I'm going to call your station so that you can accompany me back to where it happened. I'll see you in fifteen minutes!'

I began to feel sorry for Pat as I listened to him stammer out, 'Well, in view of everything you have told me, Mr Kennedy, I will have to accept that it must have been my dog that bit your son. I am so very sorry. He has never done anything like this before, I just can't understand it. I hope your son will be okay.'

I decided to allow Mr Kennedy to relieve Pat of some of his misery, 'Listen to me, Guard, as I said, I am an Assistant Secretary in the Department of Justice and, as such, I have a lot of official dealings with An Garda Síochána, an organisation for which I have the highest respect. I bear no ill will against you personally and am prepared to let the matter drop if you can assure me that, assuming you have a proper license for your dog, you will keep him under proper control.' Sheer joy poured down the line, 'Oh, thank you so much, Mr Kennedy. That is very decent of you. I assure you the dog is licensed and will be kept inside from now on. Thank you, Sir.'

With that, Mr Kennedy and his wounded child disappeared from Pat's life.

I returned to the station so that Pat could take his lunch. He met me outside, waving a piece of paper in the air, ranting and raving with the bones of the story that I had told him. I calmed him down and took the paper from him; it was a dog license. As far as he was concerned he had saved Bonzo from certain death. He even asked Kathleen, in the Post Office, to backdate the license to January 4th, just to be sure, to be sure. Off he went to his lunch and to tell the whole story all over again to Vera. Naturally his good wife informed him that Bonzo had never stepped outside the house, having spent the entire morning dozing peacefully in his basket. There was no way he had attacked anyone anywhere.

Pat came back in a foul humour, 'I've been fooled! Vera swears that Bonzo never left the house. Some smart bastard set me up and when I find out who it was he'll wish he was never born.' I had intended to confess but was taken aback by his rage. Before I could make a reply he turned for the door again, 'You stay here! I'm going over to the Post Office to see who made the call. It was the only phone call all morning so it won't take me long to find out where it came from.'

It was time to come clean, 'Don't bother, Pat. It was me, I made the call and I'm glad I did. You should be bloody well ashamed of yourself. As a member of An Garda Síochána you took an oath to uphold the law and you were too mean to buy a license but not too proud to prosecute anyone else who doesn't have a license, including the ones who don't have two pennies to rub together. How could you, knowing that you were guilty of the very same thing? It's disgusting!'

He looked like he wanted to strangle me. Instead he invoked the gods to visit a string of curses down upon my head, called me a lot of unrepeatable names, and practically took the door off its hinges when he slammed it shut behind him.

When the Sergeant returned from his holiday he was barely over the station's threshold when he had Bonzo's license thrust into his face. I sat at my desk in silence as Pat talked about being a man of his word. When he went home for lunch, Sergeant said to me, 'I could have sworn he had no intention whatsoever of buying a license. It just goes to show how you can misjudge people'. I nodded, 'Yes, Sergeant. I'm going out on my beat now but would you give Pat a message. I forgot to tell him that a Mr Kennedy phoned earlier and was sorry to have missed him. He said he'd ring back.' I watched the Sergeant write down the name in his pad and left with a smile on my face.

1952: Farnanes: The First Dance and Beauty Competition!

One day I suggested to my Sergeant, John Markey, that we should run a dance in the local hall for the Garda Benevolent Fund. 'Are you out of your mind? You'll never get anyone to support it,' was his response. I assured him that as long as it was well organised the good people of Farnanes would come out in their droves. He told me that I'd have to ask the Superintendent for his permission and remained unconvinced by my confidence.

The Super was James McKenna, a Monaghan man, a veteran of the War of Independence and a gentleman to his fingertips. He readily gave his permission and I set about organising a committee. I selected the members, wanting them to be from as varied an array of backgrounds as possible. Therefore, I chose a member of the Mill Workers Union, the local postmistress, Rose Crowley, a post man, two members of Macra ná Feirme, along with a local representative of all the political parties. Our chairman was Ted Murphy, who was a Peace Commissioner, a farmer and a former member of the London Metropolitan Police. I have to say that they made a wonderful committee, being extremely active and co-operative.

We were also going to run a Miss Crookstown Competition in conjunction with the dance, a beauty contest which as soon as it was announced generated great excitement amongst the ladies in the surrounding areas. The next thing I had to do was organise some advertising. A Detective who worked in Dublin Castle was a good friend of mine and a great artist. I asked him to do up some posters for me which he did and they proved most popular indeed. He drew an attractive lady wearing a fetching hat, with the caption: *I'm wearing my new hat to the*

Garda dance in Crookstown! It proved such a hit that drapery shops all over Cork City, Macroom and Bandon wanted posters for their windows, making it necessary to ring my friend and have my stock replenished. There were no photocopiers in those days so I reckon he must have had to draw two hundred posters in total !

The next thing I did was hire buses to run from Cork City, Macroom and Bandon. We were holding the dance on St Patrick's Night, in the Crookstown Catholic Hall, which was quite large. For entertainment I went through the papers and found an advertisement in the *Cork Examiner* for a Mr Maurice Mulcahy and his orchestra. This was to be Maurice's first engagement ever. I hired him for seventeen pounds to play from eight o'clock in the evening until two o'clock, the following morning, a more than fair price.

I decided not to provide any refreshments, neither food nor drink, alcoholic or otherwise. Other stations had held dances for the fund but, as far as I was concerned, they were more like drinking parties for the guards and their friends. I wanted to steer clear of this sort of thing. Admission was five shillings and I was fully confident that people would be happy enough to mingle and dance to the music. And I was right!

By a quarter past eight the hall was packed. It was a fantastic night. One woman told me afterwards that while dancing she lifted her foot to scratch it but the hall was so full that she didn't get her foot back down to the floor until the dance was over.

For the Miss Crookstown Competition I assembled a panel of four judges, two men and two women. The prize, of a sash and what we hoped would be a perpetual cup, went to a girl from Cork City. Her photograph ended up in the *Cork Examiner* and the *Southern Star*. It wasn't the only thing she won that night. She met a guard at the dance and they got married twelve months later.

The night was a huge success and although I cannot remember exactly how much money we raised, I know it was a substantial sum.

1953: Kilbrittain Garda Station, West Cork

Eager for promotion I had sat the examination, to progress to the rank of Sergeant, in Bandon on July 12th 1952. I cycled to Bandon where sixteen guards were hoping to get one of the two positions available. The exam was at half nine, with a break for lunch, and finished at five in the evening, a long day considering I had to cycle twelve miles there and back again.

Chief Superintendent James Dowd was the examiner. I was asked about the Larceny Act, the Malicious Damages Act and the Children's Act. Since I had studied these in great detail I was quite confident of my performance and, in fact, I got first class marks.

Nancy had given birth to our first child, John, on August 6th and we were both enjoying our new role as parents. In fact, John at the time, was the only baby in the village and as such enjoyed the attention of all the locals any time Nancy took him out in the pram.

That October I had to go to Headquarters, in Dublin, for the second part of the exam. Fifty of us were tested in drilling procedures. Thanks to my years in the LDF I got 49½ out of 50.

The results were announced that Christmas. I had passed with top marks and was now on a panel of new Sergeants just waiting to hear about a post becoming vacant to which I would be assigned. It was a great Christmas. I was awarded twenty-five pounds from the review board for good police work while Nancy's mother had sent her twenty pounds for Christmas. What with the unexpected money, our new baby and my promotion, we felt we were on the pig's back.

On 27 May 1953 I was officially promoted to the rank, pay and respect, if any, of Sergeant and received the news that I was to be transferred to Allihies, in West Cork, the next parish to America. There was to be a three-way transfer : I was going to Allihies, the Sergeant in Allihies was to go to Birdhill while the Sergeant there was being sent to Donegal. I was concerned about my new station because it was so remote. In other words, if we wanted to visit Nancy's family in Dublin it would be a long and costly journey. Fortunately, however, I had three cases pending so I wasn't free to move until July by which time everything had changed. The Sergeant in Birdhill requested to stay where he was since he was only three months away from retirement. In the midst of all this a vacancy came up in Kilbrittain and that's where I ended up.

When I first arrived in the seaside village I could not find any suitable rental accommodation available so I had to send Nancy and John back to Dublin to stay with her family until I worked something out. Meantime, my life revolved around the station in that I slept there, above the offices. I took my meals in the village café.

There were three Gardaí in the station, all senior members of An Garda Síochána, having joined the force three years before I was born. Two of them were alcoholics and due to some long standing grievances, none of them were on speaking terms with the others.

Therefore, it was with a certain feeling of trepidation that I took up duty in July acutely aware of the fact that the three Gardaí were all old enough to be my father. Here was I, a young Sergeant taking over as the 'boss' and meeting out orders to them. I could easily see the situation from their point of view and as a consequence, vowed to tread warily. In my opening remarks to the men, I did point out that I was mindful of the fact that it was them and their colleagues who had joined the force in 1922 and armed with only a baton and moral courage, in difficult times, had brought peace to the country and made life safe for guys like me.

My remarks were well received and I was warmly welcomed by the station party who pledged their loyal support to me. I told them that I was aware of the problems in the station but I needed them to work as a team and pleaded with them to bury the hatchet and shake hands. To my huge relief they agreed to do just that.

For the next while things were quite harmonious in the office. Unfortunately, the fragile peace didn't last very long.

We were paid on a monthly basis with cheques that had to be cashed in Bandon. One of my guards asked me if he could take the next set of cheques to Bandon. I agreed and put it down in the station diary in accordance with regulations. He took off on his bicycle and once he had cycled into the distance, one of his colleagues said to me, 'You know you shouldn't have let him go.'

'Why not?' I asked.

He sniffed pointedly, 'Because he is going to go and get drunk with the proceeds of the cheques and we'll be left here with no money!'

Unfortunately he was right. Three days went by without sight or sound of my messenger and our wages. I called out to his house to speak to his wife, a pleasant and practical woman, who told me that her husband's disappearance was perfectly normal behaviour. 'But the thing is, Sergeant, once he's over his binge, he won't taste a drop of drink until the next pay day.' Unfortunately, her words gave me neither consolation nor optimism.

On my way back to the station I stopped to talk to Jim, the postman. I had my back to the road so it was up to Jim to tell me, 'Oh, here's your man now and he's taking both sides of the road with him.' With that there was a crash. My missing guard was lying flat on the road, his bike on its side, the back wheel spinning righteously. His son and daughter suddenly appeared and, without a word, lifted their father off the ground and brought him home. I guessed that they had taken part in this ceremony once or twice before.

He turned up for work the next morning at nine o'clock, a sorry sight indeed. His spectacles were broken, his uniform was grubby and his face was covered in cuts and bruises. I looked at him, 'What happened to you?' He rubbed his neck, for the sake of doing something, 'The thing is, Sergeant, I just don't know.' I snapped, 'Well, I do! You were so drunk that you didn't know your own name. Let me make myself clear, I will not tolerate this behaviour'.

He nodded his head, 'I'm sorry, Sergeant, I am, but I'd be grand if only I could sleep for a little while'.

I briefly considered taking disciplinary action against him but I really didn't want to do that. He had a big family and also, I genuinely liked and respected his wife. Knowing that reporting his behaviour would most likely result in his dismissal, and cause her and her children even more problems than they currently had to deal with. So instead, I sent him to one of the rooms upstairs to sleep it off.

In future I would be more careful when delegating the cashing of the cheques. Needless to say, he was never again assigned with that particular task.

***

I had a visit at the station, one morning, from a local farmer who told me that he had been obliged to investigate a strange smell which was pervading throughout his house. He and his wife had just returned from attending the Kinsale Agricultural Show. Their maid, a sixteen year old orphan girl, was missing but they heard that she had to ring for the doctor in their absence and had been taken to the North Infirmary in Cork.

After searching all the places from which he thought might logically be the source of the smell, he finally decided that it was emanating from underneath the floor in the front room. He took up the floor boards only to make the grim discovery of the body of a new-born baby. It didn't take him or his wife long to work out who the mother was.

I accompanied him back to his house after first calling for a pathologist to meet me there. When the pathologist arrived he carried out an initial examination of the body. He removed the baby's liver and put it in water. If it floated it meant that the child itself had breathed after birth. The liver didn't float, indicating that the baby had never taken a breath on its own after birth. With the confirmation that it had been a stillbirth, we at least knew that thankfully, we did not have a murder on our hands.

A few days later I visited the girl at the Infirmary. My heart went out to her as she told me in confidence that the farmer was the father of her baby. The poor girl was distraught. She feared that she was going to end up imprisoned for what she had done and also that once her disgrace was made public, she would never find work again. Frightened that she was going to end up on the side of the road, I assured her that I would do all I could for her and implored her not to worry.

The outcome of the court case was that she was charged with concealment of a birth but I managed to arrange a special sitting before a sympathetic District Justice. I also suggested, with respect, that the probation act be applied and he willingly agreed.

Meanwhile I went back to the farmer to tell him what I had learned. I assured him that I wasn't in the business of breaking up marriages, explaining that all I wanted was two hundred pounds for the girl herself. I felt it was the least she deserved. A wealthy man, he readily agreed and gave me the money which I was delighted to be able to hand over to her. The young girl's relief was understandably huge. I am glad to say that she was able to put the sad business behind her. Before she left the infirmary she had found herself a new job working for a family in Ballinaspittle, who never knew a thing about her earlier troubles.

***

One evening, Joe, a local strong farmer came into the station in need of my help. He was a decent, upright, family man and he seemed extremely worried about something. I asked him was there something wrong. 'Yes, there is, Sergeant. I really hope you can help me.' Whatever it was it sounded serious. He took a deep breath and began, 'Do you know my daughter Eileen, Sergeant?' I said I did, she was a lovely girl of about nineteen years of age. 'Well, she's walking out with Peter Doran from the village and has told me that she wants to marry him. But me and the wife were hoping she would marry a strong farmer like myself.' Peter was a talented carpenter and had always impressed me as a thoroughly nice fellow.

Doubting my initial response that this was a serious matter I asked Joe, 'Okay, but how can I help you?' He squirmed a little before continuing, 'He comes up every Sunday and Wednesday, on his motorbike, at seven o'clock and, well, we were hoping you could come around one of those evenings and give him a beating, to put him off like.' I couldn't believe what I was hearing. 'For God's sake, Joe, my job is to preserve the peace, not beat people up. There is no way I will help you and you are not to touch him either. Am I making myself clear?' His confidence in me was shaken and he left the station looking like he had just heard the worst news possible.

Suffice to say his daughter married her hard-working carpenter a year later and never regretted her decision. As far as I remember her father never put a foot in the station again, not while I was there at any rate. I can only hope that in time he had come to accept his son-in-law and was content that, in hindsight, I hadn't agreed to comply with his strange request!

Kilbrittain was also the scene of my first case of blackmail.

On the evening of the 15 August, Tom Moore, a local and prominent farmer, called into the station to show me a letter he had received a few days earlier. He assured me that he had absolutely no idea who it was from.

The letter read:

> *Dear Father,*
>
> *I suppose you thought that I would never do this. You miserable bastard! How you wronged my mother. Before she died she told me you were my father and unless you put five hundred pounds on your wife's grave, in Bandon Cemetery, by next Friday, I am going to expose you.*
>
> *This is no idle threat!*
>
> *Signed,*
>
> *Your eldest child.*

Tom stared anxiously at me as I read the letter. I sighed, 'Do you realise the implications, Tom? The writer is accusing you of having fathered an illegitimate child. I will certainly investigate the matter but it may reveal more than you would like. In other words now is the time to tell me if there could possibly be any truth whatsoever in these words.' He shook his head, 'I have nothing to fear, Sergeant. I have only two children: Joe, my son, and daughter Mary.'

'Okay, I'll proceed with the investigation so. Will you allow me to reply to the letter on your behalf, though I promise you that I will not be using your name?' He thought for a couple of seconds before agreeing to my proposal. 'Of course, Sergeant, whatever you think is best.'

And so, I wrote out my brief reply:

> *I received your letter and am very surprised you are doing this. I don't have five hundred pounds and it will take me some time to get that much money together. I ask for your patience.*
>
> *Signed,*
>
> *You know who.*

I put my note into an envelope on the inside of which I had written my own initials, M.F.B., in writing so small as to ensure that nobody else would spot them. The following Thursday I waited until it was dark and then I placed the letter on Mrs Moore's grave, covering it over with grass and stones. I fancied that this might be the end of it.

Seven days later Tom was back in the station with another letter, still threatening to expose him if he didn't hand over the money. I replied to that one in a similar way as I had to the first, repeating the need for more time to get so much money together and, once again, wrote my initials inside the envelope.

The following Wednesday there was yet another letter, carrying the same threat but this time the five hundred pounds ransom had doubled, the blackmailer now demanding the grand total of one thousand pounds. By this stage Tom had received a total of five letters and I think he felt they would never stop. I decided it was time to begin keeping watch on the grave and see if I could apprehend the writer in the act.

On Friday evening, just after it got dark, wearing an extra overcoat in anticipation of a long, cold night ahead, I cycled over to the cemetery in Bandon where I hid my bicycle, found Mrs Moore's grave and then took up a concealed spot behind the headstone of another grave nearby. And there I remained *all* night. It wasn't at all comfortable, not least because it rained the whole night through. Also, I had not thought to bring any food or drink with me and, all in all, it was just plain strange to be spending all night in a graveyard. I dearly missed having someone to talk to but I was determined to end Tom's torment and this was the only conceivable way to do it.

As it happened there were no visitors to the grave that night. At seven o'clock on Saturday morning I cycled home after arranging for a guard from Bandon Station to take my place by the grave. Following a quick breakfast, wash and change of clothes I jumped on my bicycle and was back at the grave for ten o'clock, allowing my relief to return to his station. I settled down to hide behind the same headstone, making sure I had full view of Tom's wife's grave.

It seemed like only a few minutes later I had my reward for the previous night's unpleasantness when a woman entered the cemetery and walked straight up to Mrs Moore's grave. Apart from anything else I was hugely relieved as I began to worry that I might have to spend a second or even third night crouched behind a headstone. I recognised her immediately. It was Mary Ward from the next village. Making sure I had my culprit, I waited as she sat down on the grave, retrieved my last letter from under the stones and opened it up to read. Sneaking up behind her I snatched the letter from her hand and asked in a loud, stern voice, 'What are you doing here?'

To her credit she came up with a story immediately, 'I met a man on the road to Bandon and he told me that he would pay me to collect a letter from Mrs Moore's grave.' I stared at her but she never blinked, and ordered her to describe him. Again she answered me quickly, 'Well, I'd say he's about thirty years of age with dark hair, and he was wearing blue overalls and wellington boots.' In any case I arrested her and took her to Bandon Garda Station. There, she repeatedly denied that she had anything to do with the actual sending of the letters.

The next thing I had to do was get a search warrant and see if my plan worked. Detective Sergeant Pat McKenna accompanied me, with warrant in hand, out to Mary's house where we met considerable opposition from her mother and father regarding making a search of their home. However, they had no choice in the matter and grudgingly stood aside to allow us to move through the interior of the house which was spotlessly clean and tidy. I recall remarking that even the socks were folded neatly in their drawers.

I struck gold in the kitchen when I opened a drawer and found a writing pad. From the indentations on the blank page I could clearly make out the date of the last letter which had been sent. A further search produced all the letters I had written, my initials on the envelopes presenting concrete evidence of their origin. Making polite conversation with Mrs Ward, I congratulated her on her perfectly kept house. She answered me proudly, 'That's down to my daughter, Sergeant. The way you rear them is the way you'll have them!' I could make no sensible reply to this.

When we returned to the station I charged Mary under section 31 of the Larceny Act 1916, for demanding money with menace from Tom Moore. I gave her a legal caution while she remained silent. She was brought to a special court and temporarily released on her father's bail until her next court date when she was further remanded for one month.

Sometime later, we all ended up in the Circuit Court in Cork City in front of a judge and jury. The trial lasted three days with me spending a day and half in the witness box. Fortunately I had more than my initialled envelopes to offer the Judge as evidence. It transpired that six people had seen Mary on the road that Saturday morning, on her way to the cemetery, and not one of them saw her talk to a thirty year old man in overalls and wellingtons.

The jury took forty-five minutes to return the verdict, "Guilty as Charged". Mary received a suspended sentence of twelve months in prison. For my part, the judge complimented me on two counts, the way I had presented the evidence in my case and also for my detecting abilities and my idea of initialling those envelopes.

1956: Kilbrittain Garda Station, West Cork; a Challenging Inspection

In the month of June, 1956 an Assistant Commissioner was making a tour of inspection in the division of West Cork and we were notified that the station in Kilbrittain was included in his itinerary of inspections.

The station itself was far from what could be described as salubrious. Most of the furniture had been leftover from the days when the station was run by the RIC (Royal Irish Constabulary) and without doubt showed its age. Since I had arrived, in an effort to give the station something of a face lift, I had saved money from the station's cleaning, fuel and electricity allowance and used it to buy lino for the floor of the public office, curtains for the two windows and a cloth to cover the table which had endured many years of scratches, pen marks and general wear and tear. I also had painted all the chairs a dark mahogany colour and slowly over time, I had transformed the office from a bare, sombre place into something a lot more friendly and welcoming

On the morning of the inspection I added a few more homely touches, bringing a Waterford crystal vase from home, filling it with flowers. When the Assistant Commissioner arrived at the door he briefly looked into the Public Office and completely missed myself and the rest of the station party who were assembled there, standing to attention. On reflection, I think that when he saw the flowers, curtains and table cloth he assumed it was the married quarters and so, he took a left which brought him into the tiny kitchen. I dutifully gave a little cough and he retraced his footsteps back to where we were. Typically, his gruff greeting was, 'So this is where you are hiding!' For some reason he felt moved to pull back the table cloth. On seeing the ink stains he huffed, 'You should wash your dirt, Sergeant. Don't try to hide it.' I bit my lip in annoyance.

'Now', he said, turning to one of the Gardaí, 'What's your name?'

'Guard Quinlan, Sir'.

The guard was a Kerryman, and with all respect to his fellow natives, they are noted for their love of the evasive answer. The conversation continued thus:

'Where were you stationed before Kilbrittain?'

'In Limerick, Sir'.

'What part of Limerick?'

'West Limerick'.

'Where in West Limerick?'

'In Pallas District, Sir'.

'What station in Pallas District?'

'Doon'.

As it happened, the Assistant Commissioner had previously been a Chief in Limerick. His next question was rather pointed, 'Aren't you the guard that was caught poaching pheasants in Doon?'

'Yes, Sir'.

Satisfied with this interview he turned to my second colleague, asking him where he had been stationed?'

'At Allihies, Sir.'

The Assistant Commissioner had also been Chief in Bandon, and once again was able to place the guard, 'Indeed you were in Allihies and every other station in West Cork. Did you give up the drink yet?'

The reply was immediate if not terribly precise, 'Well, more or less, Sir'.

Happy to have proved himself somewhat, he turned to me, 'I'll see the rooms now, Sergeant'.

There were two rooms upstairs, each with a built-in wardrobe. In one of the wardrobes I kept a large cardboard box for wastepaper. I hadn't thought to do anything about it since it was well out of the way and I hadn't for a moment though that it would feature in the inspection. We went upstairs and sure enough he asked me to open the door of the wardrobe. When he saw the box I suffered a minor interrogation of my own.

'What's in the box, Sergeant?'

'Nothing, Sir.'

'And what is it hiding?'

'Nothing, Sir.'

'Pull it out.'

When I complied with his order a small spider's web was revealed to be clinging to the corner of the wardrobe.

Sure enough he spotted it immediately and of course he thought it worthy of comment, 'More of your dirt, Sergeant!' By this stage, I was beginning to wonder if maybe the station was actually covered in filth that I had never noticed!

The floorboards in the next room contained quite a number of black timber knots. There was an audible gasp before the Assistant Commissioner managed to ask, 'When did *she,* (meaning our cleaner), last clean that floor? Whenever it was, she used damned dirty water!'

I replied, 'I don't know, Sir. I was out on patrol when she was here.'

His next question really nettled me, 'Would you like to eat your dinner off that floor, Sergeant?'

I didn't answer.

'Are you deaf, Sergeant? I asked you if you would like to eat your dinner off that floor.'

Bristling with indignation, I took a deep breath, 'Thank God, Sir, I am not deaf. I am lucky enough to have all my faculties but I do resent, in the strongest possible terms, your extremely offensive question. In truth I didn't have a lot before joining the Garda Síochána and I certainly don't have much more now. However, I would never stoop so low as to eat my dinner off the floor.'

'Oh', he said, 'Smart boy!'

We went downstairs for the examination of police duties, that is, in regard to our knowledge of the law. It was part of every station's inspection. I had already chosen a topic on which my two guards would be questioned, The Road Traffic Act 1933. On hearing my choice he groaned loudly, 'Oh, for God's sake, Sergeant. I am hearing the same bloody thing in every other station. Can you not think of something else?'

Tiring of his negative attitude towards my station, I made a potentially unwise choice, 'As far as I'm concerned, Sir, I could choose any act from the Garda Síochána Guide (our law book). He was surprised, 'So, we really have a smart boy here. Okay, ask them whatever you like.'

If he was surprised, it was nothing compared to the shock on my colleagues' faces. They knew very little about any acts. Actually it was a constant surprise to me to realise how little they knew, despite the fact they had been enforcing the laws for the last thirty years or so. Thinking on my feet, I took up my position behind the Assistant Commissioner's chair and proceeded to ask questions that only required either a yes or no answer. If the answer was yes I'd nod my head, if it was no I'd shake my head. It was the perfect plan except that the good man copped on to what I was doing. When I asked the next question, he said, 'Why don't you just answer it for them, since that's what you've been doing so far.'

Examination over, he looked through our record book. Reading that the station had successfully dealt with each of its fifteen indictable offences he commented, 'A lot of crimes for a tuppence halfpenny place like Kilbrittain.'

In his report he made just one derogatory comment; that the barrack furniture should and could be cleaner.

Relieved that his visit had finally come to an end I accompanied him to his car, which was parked outside the station, facing east. His next port of call was Timoleague and he asked me in what direction it was. I answered the question I was asked, 'It's west of here, Sir.' He snapped impatiently, 'Don't be doing the f***king Corkman on me. Tell me how I get there?' Unwilling to let him away with anything at this point, I said, 'Why didn't you ask me that question in the first instance, Sir?' Before he could reply, I added, 'Tell your driver to turn the car around and take the first left which will bring you straight to Timoleague. The station is just past the church, on the left.'

When I walked back into the station the two guards were waiting for me. All smiles, they shook my hand. 'Thanks be to Jesus', said Garda

Quinlan, 'that I lived to see the day that someone was man enough to stand up to that lousy f***king bastard!' I laughed. 'Now', he continued, 'neither you nor I take a drink but let's all go over to Simms's Pub and have a couple of bottles of lemonade to celebrate.' It was a brilliant suggestion and the three of us headed across the street in great humour. Quinlan and I enjoyed our two bottles of lemonade before returning to work. The second Guard, the one who had been stationed all over West Cork, went on drinking, and I can assure you it wasn't lemonade. We didn't see him for the next three days. Obviously in his case, less was more!

***

It was a Saturday morning in May 1956 and I had taken the day off to drive my family to Cork. I got up early and went down to the station to make sure everything was okay before we headed off. When I returned home Nancy told me that she had had a terrible dream about a local farmer called Ned Maloney. She dreamt he died after his tractor overturned on his way back from the creamery. She was a bit shaken but I was able to reassure her that he was alive and well. I had just seen him driving by on his tractor. We thought no more about it.

However, her dream, as shocking as this may sound, turned out to be prophetic in a way. Just before we left for Cork I got a call that there had been a bad traffic accident. Another young lad we knew was driving his tractor in Glanduff when it mounted the fence on the left side of the road and overturned, pinning him to the ground. He was dead by the time I arrived on the scene. The road he was on would have allowed him to see huge liners on their way to Cobh. I later learned that one such liner would have been passing around the time of the accident. They were impressive sights to behold and you could often hear the music that was being played on the ship. What I feel might have happened is that the liner caught the driver's attention who probably marvelled at its size, completely losing his focus on his driving.

It was a particularly sad story since the boy's mother was a widow and he was her only child. I'll always remember the beautiful summer's day, the sun shining brightly from a clear blue sky and the sound of the birds merrily singing as the mother came along the road and howled in agony when she understood what had happened. I don't think I will ever forget that woman's sorrow. It remains one of the worst experiences I ever had throughout my entire career.

1957: The Chase is on

It was about seven o'clock on a summer's evening when I had a visitor to the station in the form of John McCarthy, from Killeshin which was about three miles from Kilbrittain. In his heyday John had been a terrific runner, winning plenty of trophies, and was, therefore known locally as "Johnny the Champ". These days he was a popular carpenter. However he had not come in to the station to make a social call but, it transpired, had called to report a break in. While he was out at work someone had forced open his barn door and made off with a horse's bridle and saddle, along with a copper spraying machine.

Nancy had taken the children back to Dublin to stay with her family, so as to avoid the perils of a bad outbreak of polio which had recently become rampant throughout West Cork. This meant that I was free to go straight out to make house to house enquiries, to see if any of the neighbours had noticed any strangers in the area that day. At every house I learned that sometime between three and four o'clock, in the afternoon, two young traveller gentlemen had knocked at the door looking for scrap. I ended up with a good and full description of the pair. I was looking for two boys travelling by pony and trap. The trap was painted a noticeably vibrant green colour and the pony was a piebald. A bicycle was tied to the back of the trap. With this information I went off to visit the halting sights on the southern side of the district. I had always made it my business to get to know who was on the sites and to maintain a good relationship with them. Unfortunately, despite their willingness to be of help, nobody there had any information which would help me with my enquiries.

It was gone midnight by the time I got home and when I finally settled down for some well-earned shut eye, I set my alarm clock for seven o'clock. The next morning, after a quick breakfast, I cycled over to the halting sites on the northern side but again failed to obtain any useful information. I suppose realistically, it was a bit much to expect any of the travellers I asked to help me catch one of their own. After that I cycled to Bandon where I had a good lunch for four shillings. As I came out of the café there was a woman looking in a shop window. We got chatting and she told me she was from Ballineen which was seven miles west of Bandon. In conversation, I described the green trap and the two travellers. To my relief she responded immediately, 'Oh, my goodness. I know who you mean. I was hanging out clothes last evening and they passed by, heading west'.

I realised that I couldn't follow them on my bicycle so I popped into the garda station and asked Detective Ned Bracken, the driver of the station's patrol car, to help me out. Ned drove us to Skibbereen, we arrived there about eight in the evening, having stopped at houses along the road, to ensure that the travellers had indeed come this way. Every resident that we spoke to could verify that they had knocked on their door looking for scrap. Of course we knew we were definitely on the right path when we saw the green trap and piebald pony tied to a lamp post in Skibbereen. There was no sign of the travellers but John McCarthy's possessions were sitting in the back of the trap. I called into a shop that was still open and the elderly lady behind the counter told me that she was absolutely sure that she had earlier seen the two fellows go into the cinema across the road.

Finding it hard to believe that our two boys had found the time during their spree to stop off to catch the latest blockbuster, we nonetheless went into the cinema and easily found them even in the darkness. Apologising to the rest of the bemused patrons for interrupting their viewing, we hauled them outside. I took out my notebook and asked for their names. John Carberry was nineteen years of age and Tony Driscoll, his partner in crime, was two years older. We marched them over to the trap. Pointing at the saddle, bridle and spraying machine, I asked, 'These are stolen goods. Can either of you explain why they are in your trap?' Neither of them looked particularly upset to be confronted by two guards and I guessed that this probably wasn't their first time to find themselves in such a situation. 'Oh, jaysus!' bawled Tony, 'Who put them there? Some dirty bastard has set us up and no mistake!' Far from impressed with his poor attempt at a logical explanation of the situation, I promptly arrested himself and his business partner.

We put the stolen property into the boot of the car and brought them to the station in Skibbereen where they were charged with house-breaking and larceny of property. A Peace Commissioner was asked to hold a special court in the station and, at my request, he remanded the boys in custody to Cork Jail to appear the following Friday at Bandon District Court.

We drove them straight to Cork Jail. I sat in the back of the car, Tony handcuffed to my right hand and John handcuffed to my left. It was a most uncomfortable journey as I was sure that one or both of them were highly likely to make a run for it. Ned and I deposited them in jail and we drove back to Bandon. I collected my bike and we got back to my house at seven in the morning, having been out all night. We were both starving and I was delighted to remember that I had a cooked chicken in the larder. I brought Ned in and we made a meal of it.

The following Friday the two travellers were sentenced to six months imprisonment. It was hugely satisfactory to get the thieves in the end, thereby solving the crime and returning the stolen property to its rightful owner. I have often thought afterwards of the hours of overtime I had put in to solve the case, without so much as a thought that had overtime been paid for in those days, I would have made a fortune! For me at the time, the satisfaction of a successful outcome was reward enough.

1957: My First Car

I was enjoying a day off, working out in the garden. Nancy came out at about three o'clock with coffee and home-made scones and I sat down to savour them in the sun. When I was finished I suddenly exclaimed for no particular reason, 'You know something love, I think it's time we bought a car!' Nancy was unmoved, 'With what, buttons?' I laughed, 'No, with money!' She looked at me, 'and where are you going to get this money?' I shrugged, 'From the bank!' It took me all day to convince her that it was a practical plan, both to buy a car and to borrow money from the bank to do so; she had a terrible fear of debt and the idea of having the burden of repaying a loan to a formidable institution like a bank was quite unappealing to her to say the least.

In truth, there was much to recommend the idea. A car would make our life a lot easier, especially in relation to visiting our families. At this point when we wanted to visit Leitrim we had to hire a car in Kilbrittain for fifteen shillings to take us to Bandon where we had to take a bus to Cork City, to get the train to Dublin where we had to stay overnight because the train to the west had already left. The next morning we got on the train at Westland Row, got off at Dromod to take the narrow-gauge train to Mohill, from where we took a hackney cab to Cloone. It was an exhausting and expensive trip. Surely it was no wonder I was longing to buy a car.

There were two banks in Bandon, The Munster and Leinster Bank, (M&L), and the Bank of Ireland, (BOI). I knew both of the managers personally as I kept an eye on their summer properties at Harbour View, (which was in my district), when they were away. I visited the M&L to talk to Joe Riordan. He welcomed me into his office, 'Well, Michael how can I help you?' I told him that I wanted two hundred and fifty pounds to buy a second-hand car. He threw his two hands in the air. 'Oh, Michael, I am so sorry but I couldn't possible lend you that kind of money to buy a car, it's simply unprofitable for us. I do hope you understand that my hands are tied'. I shook his tied hands and left feeling that I had learned a couple of valuable lessons.

I went down the street to the BOI to talk to Manager George Wilson. When he asked, 'Well, Michael, what can I do for you?' I was more than ready having had my card marked by my earlier visit to his competitor up the road. 'I do hope you can help me. You see my father-in-law is in the dairy business up in Dublin and he told me that he has a lot of extra grass this year. He wants me to buy five yearlings and he will look after them, fatten them up for me, and then I can sell them on for a good profit'. George was immediately interested, 'How much are yearlings?' Again I was ready for this question. 'Well, my father-in-law says I would need three hundred pounds but I do have fifty pounds in the Post Office so I'd only need a loan of two hundred and fifty pounds'. I felt it was important to show him I was a thrifty sort of person, the fifty pounds did not exist – I hadn't a blessed penny to my name – but I figured that it was unlikely that he would actually check this out for himself.

George thought for a moment before asking, 'and how would you pay us back?' My answer was immediate and confident, as if I had given it plenty of thought before arriving into his office, 'once a month without fail!' He only had the authority to lend me a hundred pounds so he had to check with Head Office about the two hundred and fifty pounds. A few days later a letter arrived at the house to inform me that the Bank of Ireland was lending us two hundred and fifty pounds. Delighted with myself I showed the letter to Nancy who immediately asked, 'Yes, but how are we going to pay it back?' I patted her on the arm, 'Ah, we'll cross that bridge when we come to it'.

I bought a Standard 8 car for two hundred and ten pounds, (to this day I still remember the registration number, ZT 3516). The owner wanted two hundred and thirty for it but after some negotiation, he eventually dropped his price. The tax cost me six pounds and the insurance was eleven pounds. Sure enough, I crossed the bridge of the repayments, managing to set aside enough money each month to cover the agreed amount. Nancy learned to drive the car and it made a huge difference to our lives. A few years later when we were leaving Kilbrittain I sold it on for a hundred and ninety pounds. It was a wonderful investment. I think a person's first car will always be the most important car that they will ever own, no matter what they go on to drive in later years. That first car is the one they will care for and appreciate the most.

***

1958: First Communion Blues, Kilbrittain

Life in Kilbrittain was good. The community was one into which we had easily settled, as the people were warm, welcoming and helpful. We had great friends and neighbours who never made us feel like the proverbial "blow-ins", in fact so much so that it was difficult to remember having ever lived anywhere else.

The only fly in the ointment so to speak was the fact that money always seemed to be tight, although our household was not unique in this regard. By this time, two more children had arrived, Anne and three years later, Gretta. As a Sergeant with six years' service in the rank, I was earning six pounds and ten shillings a week, not much to meet the overheads of a growing family. To further complicate financial matters, John our eldest child, was making his communion that year which necessitated a new suit, shoes and all the other trappings befitting such a solemn occasion. To tell the truth, I was at my wits end wondering how I was going to fund it all.

One night I was on a 'rising patrol'. We were obliged to perform three such patrols a month, between the hours of midnight and six o'clock in the morning. As you might imagine it was a quiet enough shift, some nights you wouldn't meet a soul. However, if I passed a house and the lights were on I would make sure to drop in, in case there was some kind of emergency and perhaps a doctor was needed. Moreover it was also, I felt, a perfect opportunity to maintain good public relations. The most common emergency was usually a cow about to calve, but more often than not it was merely late night visitors staying on for a game of cards.

On this particular night, at about one in the morning, I found myself down at Harbour View where, despite my financial worries, I was enjoying the scene before me. The night sky was clear allowing a full moon to shower the bay in shimmering light. From where I stood I could clearly make out the comforting flash from the lighthouse at the Old Head of Kinsale. In the distance I spied a rainbow of lights that belonged to a liner that was just starting out on its journey to America. My toe tapped in time to the music being played for the passengers. How I wished I had a camera to capture and hold onto this moment forever. It was great to be alive and maybe my rush of gratitude for the world and everyone in it allowed the Holy Spirit to suddenly inspire me with a wonderful scheme for making some extra money to cover the cost of the forthcoming communion.

I finished my shift at three and rushed home in excitement to Nancy who was, naturally enough, fast asleep. However I soon woke her – by accident of course, to share with her the details of my financial brainwave. 'What's wrong?' she asked. 'I have solved all our problems. I know how we can pay for John's Communion clothes.' Her eyes widened, 'How?' I announced my economic plan, 'I'm going to sow lettuce in my patch and sell it at the market'.

My "patch" was my share of the small garden attached to the station which was divided equally between my two colleagues and myself, giving us a third each to garden as we pleased. My wife did not share my excitement, 'For God's sake! You woke me up to tell me this? Shut up and let me go back to sleep'.

The next morning over breakfast I worked hard at convincing Nancy that my proposal was a viable proposition. I explained that for two shillings, or maybe less, I could buy sufficient lettuce seed to fill my portion of the shared garden. Apart from keeping it clear of weeds, all it would need was an occasional watering and hey presto, let nature take its course and in due time I would have a healthy crop of lettuce for sale. It would be a once off, I'd make a killing, get out quickly and John would be well kitted out for his communion.

Being an astute and cautious lady, Nancy inquired as to how I proposed to grow lettuce under the nose of my authorities and hope to avoid being taken to task on a disciplinary charge. I explained to her that it wasn't an offence to grow produce, the only offence would be committed if there was evidence of a sale. I assured her that I would take good care that such evidence would not be readily available. In any case, I'm a born optimist and firmly believe that such bridges are only to be to crossed when you come to them.

The Gods were kind to me as weather conditions were very favourable and it was with great excitement that I watched the first seedlings break ground and with the passing weeks the leaves developed into small heads. By the end of the second week of March the heads were developing well. With a bit of luck, I would have lettuce for sale by the third week in April. With the communion not due to take place until the second Sunday in May, the schedule was going to plan.

On Easter Saturday at 6.45 am, I headed off to the market in Cork City with the car laden down with the fruits of my labour, I had so big a crop that I even had boxes tied to the roof of the car. Luck was really on my side as when I touched down in the market an hour later, to my delight I noticed that amongst all the other traders with their crops of potatoes, cabbage, turnips, parsnips etc., I was the sole purveyor of lettuce ! Sales were brisk and as I didn't have any competition I was able to set my price at eight shillings a dozen heads as my first customer eagerly offered to take, fifteen dozen ! I couldn't believe my ears. That sale alone would yield me six pounds, which alone would easily cover the cost of John's suit.

My next customer took ten dozen heads and so it continued until the last dozen had been disposed of and all within just half an hour of my arrival at the market. My takings for the day amounted to the grand total of thirty eight pounds, seven shillings and six pence!

I will never forget that Saturday afternoon when I arrived home from the market. I fixed a mournful expression on my face as Nancy met me at the door, asking anxiously, 'Did you sell?' 'Sell my foot!' I groaned, 'I had to throw the whole lot in the Ballinhassing dump.'

'Oh, my God!' she gasped, 'We're ruined!' It wasn't fair to torture her any longer, 'Sit down there, love, and put out your hand.' She did what I told her to and then came my big moment, counting out those thirty eight pounds and change into the palm of her hand. To my dying day I will always remember her look of pure delight as she hugged and kissed me. Thanks to my horticultural endeavours, John's First Holy Communion Day saw him turned out so well in a lovely suit. Furthermore, I had done so well that we even had sufficient funds left over to enjoy a short holiday.

There is always a sting in the tail, however good a story is, and so it was with the growing of the lettuce.

Around the beginning of May I received a communication from the Chief Superintendent in Bandon, to the effect that Assistant Commissioner Joe Donnelly would be making a tour of inspection of the stations in the West Cork division, as per an attached schedule. Accordingly he would be visiting my station at eleven o'clock in the morning, on the twentieth of the month. The Chief added a footnote, pointing out that Mr Donnelly was a keen gardener and, therefore, would be expecting the station garden to be neatly tilled and free of weeds. My heart missed a beat on reading this. Since selling off my lettuce I had hardly glanced at my patch and, as a result, the only crop in my plot was an assortment of very healthy weeds. I imagined that if the Assistant Commissioner was to be treated to that fine spectacle, he was going to be far from impressed. Was the lettuce going to be my ruination? How on earth was I going to rectify the situation in this short time?

On 19 May, the day before the visit, I took my shovel and got to work, turning all the weeds upside down, making neat ridges in the soil and taking great care to ensure that all evidence of neglect was well camouflaged. Fortunately I am a bit of a hoarder so I had quite an abundance of empty seed packets from the seeds I had planted in my own garden, at home. Having put a number of short sticks at intervals between the drills, on top of each stick I attached an empty seed packet, each one indicating that underneath had been planted a series of different vegetables. What a transformation! I was so proud of my work that I had to remind myself that even if I was to wait until the proverbial cows came home, not one vegetable was ever likely to raise its head above the soil.

The day of the visit arrived and I checked over the garden, satisfied that everything, on the surface at least, was in order. About ten minutes before the Assistant Commissioner was due to arrive I received a phone call from the Chief Superintendent in Bandon, telling me that Mr Donnelly had to postpone his inspection owing to having to make a hasty return to Dublin to have a tooth extracted. When I put down the phone I exclaimed, 'The man has gone back to Dublin for a tooth extraction. Aren't there good enough dentists in Clonakilty, Bandon and Cork City? Could he not have his tooth out in one of those places?'

Mr Donnelly's inspection was re-scheduled for the following week. That morning, once again, I got busy with my shovel taking action against the fresh crop of weeds which had flourished since my first offensive. By the time I was finished everything was once again ship shape, all ready for the Assistant Commissioner.

A few minutes before he was due the phone rang, ominously so, I thought. It was the Chief Superintendent asking if Mr Donnelly had arrived yet. 'No, Sir, but I am expecting him any moment now.' He directed me that as soon as he arrived, I was to inform him of the sudden death of his mother at 9.30 that morning. Sad news indeed and I was certain that on receipt of this news, that once again, he would postpone his inspection leaving me once again to enter into the fray in my war of the weeds.

At that moment the gentleman in question finally appeared at the front door. As instructed I immediately told him about his mother, offering my condolences, 'May I, on my own behalf and behalf of the station party, offer you, Sir, our sincere sympathy.' He looked me straight in the eye and replied, 'Sergeant, she died of old age. I'd like to see your garden now'. His reaction rather shocked me. 'My God', I thought, not even a 'Lord have mercy on her soul' from her own son. I did my best to conceal my dismay and asked him to follow me outside. On the way to the garden Mr Donnelly, the supposedly keen gardener, glanced into the adjoining field which was full of sugar beet and remarked, 'Those potatoes are growing well, Sergeant'. At this point, I relaxed a little ahead of his expected scrutiny of my garden.

In fact my two colleagues had potatoes in their sections of the garden but Mr Donnelly only gave them a cursory glance, stopping at the edge of my own plot, to ask, 'Who has this bit?' 'It's mine, Sir'.

'So, what have you planted here, Sergeant?'

I took a deep breath and named every type of vegetable that came to mind. He nodded gravely, commenting, 'It's a credit to you'. As we headed back indoors to inspect the record keeping system, I could almost hear the mocking laughter of the subterranean crop of weeds beneath the soil !

The Assistant Commissioner duly wrote up our visit in his Inspection Minute Book:

Sergeant Bohan is administering the affairs of his sub-district on sound and common-sense lines. Eleven indictable offences, such as larcenies, house-breaking and such like have all been detected, and summary offences, (such as missing tax or insurance on cars, or lights on bicycles) are receiving due attention. His garden is neatly tilled and planted in great variety. My sincere congratulations to him.

1958: The Farmer Who Cried Wolf

There was one farmer in Kilbrittain who was the bane of my life for a number of years. Joseph Quinlan came from West Cork and had been given a land commission farm of thirty acres. He was married to Joan and they were – forgive me – both as thick as wooden planks. They had two children, a thirteen year old son and a twelve year old daughter. To his credit, Joseph was a hard-working farmer and in time he acquired two other farms to add to his first one, giving him a grand total of ninety acres of land.

Unfortunately for his neighbours, Joe's motto was: a borrower or lender I'll never be. Therefore, it will be no surprise to learn that he was far from popular in the community which resulted in some of his outer buildings being subjected to a bout of stone-throwing from local youths. Windows were broken but I did catch at least one culprit in the act. They would also open the gates to the fields, so that Joe's cows would end up strolling merrily along the roads.

One night I was at home and was just sitting down to enjoy the tea which Nancy had prepared, when Joe and his wife flung themselves into our kitchen, both sobbing hysterically, saying the same thing, 'The well is poisoned!, the well is poisoned!' By now I knew not to jump to their conclusions about anything. I asked them how they knew their well had been tampered with. Joe looked grief-stricken, 'Joan got a pain after drinking her tea.' I took a deep breath, 'Did the whole family drink tea from the same water?' I was not surprised to hear the answer, 'Yes!' Glancing from one to the other I asked the obvious question, 'Well, did anyone else get sick?' Again the answer was only what I expected to hear, 'No!'

It took a few minutes but eventually I got them to leave without me, having explained to them that had the well really been poisoned, the outcome would have been more extreme than one member of the family suffering what was likely nothing more than a bout of indigestion!

I had a few months of peace before their next "episode". Joe came sprinting into the station one afternoon, shrieking, 'Help! Help! The pig's been stolen!' I steeled myself for this latest bout of histrionics, took a deep breath, told Joe to calm down and start from the beginning. Upon further questioning it transpired that his sow had given birth to twelve piglets. His son had let her out for a run around the previous evening while he cleaned out the sty. When he finished he let the pigs back in, made sure they were okay and locked the door behind him. The next morning he counted only eleven piglets with the mother. Feeling weary of the hysteria I asked him did he not think the likeliest solution was that the sow ate it, it was a common occurrence. He wouldn't hear of this, 'No! No! This is her fifth litter. It's been stolen!' I persisted as calmly as I could, 'But isn't it possible that she did eat it?' Joe was having none of it, 'I'm going to Bandon for the Superintendent!' And off he went.

I went over to his house, taking a young garda with me. His son showed us around. The door of the piggery faced the main road. Of course there was no evidence of any break-in or robbery. Joe arrived to tell me that the Superintendent was going to make a visit the following day. I pretended to believe this. Meanwhile an idea was forming in my head. What was needed was a plausible scenario to convince Joe the pig had not been stolen otherwise I knew this complaint was going to run and run. First I asked my colleague to take Joe around the back of the hayshed, telling him I had a little job to do. Next I went out to the front of the piggery, the ground was nice and mucky and I used my fingers to make little track marks from the pig sty to the road, about fifty yards worth of them. There was a big gullet at the end of Joe's land that led into an overgrown glen. When I was finished I went back for Joe and his wife, and pointed out the supposed "pig prints" in the dirt. Like a greyhound on the scent of a rabbit, Joe took off after them, finding himself at the edge of the glen. 'Ah, Sergeant! It's no use. The pig must have got out and got lost in the glen. We'll never find it!' I congratulated myself on a job well done as I checked with him, 'So, you are satisfied now that he has not been stolen?' 'Yes, Sergeant'.

Once he was happy I let him have it. 'Now, you have wasted police time in Kilbrittain. Do you realise I could prosecute you for that? It is a serious offence. Well, this time I won't but consider this your warning. And while I'm at it, you need to have a better relationship with your neighbours. If you did, you wouldn't have half of the trouble you imagine you have. It's up to you.' I turned on my heel and left that farm and, until the day I left Kilbrittain, I never heard another peep out of him. Sometimes, the most tedious police work involves no crime at all!

1959: The shooting of the harrier dogs

There was a very good harrier club in Kilbrittain, with a total of fifty-two dogs on its books. A harrier dog is a cross-country runner that is used to hunt hares and foxes. It resembles an English foxhound but is smaller in size. The local priest, Father McKeever, was chairman of the club. When I first arrived in Kilbrittain he did his utmost to encourage me to join the club, advising me it was equivalent to belonging to a sodality (a brotherhood or fraternity) in the parish. I didn't take up any of his invitations, however, since I found him to be a rather headstrong individual who was clearly used to getting his way in all matters. I figured it was probably best not to get too involved with someone of such influence and sway in the parish.

To give you an example of the kind of person he was, he arrived at the station one Monday morning needing a passport so that he could fly to Lourdes for a pilgrimage on the Friday. I told him it was very short notice but that I would do what I could, with no promises of success. I explained what I needed from him, asking for two recent photographs in the specific size required, his birth certificate, to prove his identity, along with a postal order for thirty shillings. I was slightly bewildered when he arrived back at the station with an old photograph taken when he was a curate. For one thing the photograph was too big, measuring almost six inches by four and for another it pictured him sitting on a horse!

'Father, I'm afraid this won't do. It's not the right size and they won't accept the horse'.

'What?' he asked, 'Sure everyone knows that's me!'

It took a while but I finally persuaded him to go and get me better photographs. Eventually he complied. I made my phone calls, sent everything off and got him his passport by Friday. It was an achievement in itself. However, when I rang Father McKeever to tell him that I had managed to get him sorted, instead of thanking me for my administrative miracle, he told me that he had changed his mind and was no longer going to Lourdes.

The harrier club was always in need of funds to license its dogs so every year they held a dance in order to raise money. This year it was decided to hold the dance on Easter Sunday night in the small parochial hall. There was trouble almost immediately. I didn't think they had picked the best week to hold a dance, it being Holy Week. Father McKeever complained about the timing since he was holding a mission week. Also he wouldn't drop his rates to rent out the parochial hall for the evening, which meant that a large chunk of the profits from the dance was gone before it even started, so the club felt they had no choice but to move the event to Foley's Hall in Timoleague. This upset Father McKeever even further. On Easter Sunday he complained to anyone who would listen that the club were deliberately holding the dance in opposition to his own mission week which was untrue. The mission was closing at half-past seven on Easter Sunday night and the dance was only starting an hour later at half eight. Furthermore, the people in the harrier club were good people; at least four of them had brothers who were priests so the idea of their deliberately obstructing his endeavours just wasn't logical.

Two of the harrier dogs in the club were on loan to Father McKeever himself. In fact they were the best of the fifty-two dogs because he was the chairman and therefore figured that as such, he was entitled to the best of the pack. On Easter Monday he put the two dogs in his car, along with his shot gun, and told his curate to get in too. He drove the car to the forest, handed the gun to the curate and ordered him to shoot the dogs. The timid curate felt he had no option but to comply and duly despatched the innocent animals.

I heard about this the following morning. It was a few minutes before one o'clock and I was asleep in bed. The doorbell rang, waking me up and I opened the bedroom window to find Paddy Manning, the secretary of the harrier club, on my doorstep. There were three other men with him. It was quite a crowd considering the hour. 'What's wrong, Paddy?' I asked. Paddy replied, 'Can you come down for a chat?' I was bewildered, 'But it's almost one in the morning!' With that, Paddy blurted out, 'Father McKeever has shot two of our best dogs!' He broke down crying. I quickly got dressed and ran down the stairs.

A meeting had been hastily called in the house next door. When I got there I found fifteen club members squeezed into the small living room. Every single one of them was disgusted with their chairman and without exception, they were calling for him to be prosecuted.

I had never previously encountered any similar kind of situation and was none too sure of the implications of prosecuting a priest. My gut told me that it would not be a good thing for the parish in general so I set about trying to calm the situation. They were all looking to me for a response. I took to the floor, 'Look, I agree that it was a terrible, terrible thing that he did but you have to remember that this is holy Ireland. If you prosecute a priest, all you'll end up doing is gaining him the sympathy of people who don't understand what has gone on. If you take my advice you won't persist with this. That way you will retain the support of the parish and I can guarantee that you will get more than the price of the two dogs.'

They all listened and then agreed with this, all except for one, Dan McGarty. He worked in one of the local shops and was from Ballydehob in West Cork. However, I thought it had all been settled when Dan said, 'Okay, Sergeant Bohan, but we are going to write to the priest and tell him that there are men in this parish who would like to see him punished for what he has done.'

'Dan', I said, 'Like myself you're a runner in, (not from the village), here. I suggest you take my advice and just forget about it.'

And that was that. Only, it wasn't.

The next day two carloads of club members left the village. I had it on good authority who was in the cars and where they were going. A solicitor who had fallen out with Father McKeever had invited them to come in to see him, promising them that he could get them the price of the two dead dogs, (fifty pounds each), and more.

Paddy came to see me again, telling me he wanted an investigation into the shooting and he wanted Father McKeever prosecuted. I looked at him, 'But I thought we discussed all this!' Paddy shrugged, 'We changed our minds.' 'Yes!' I said, 'since you spoke to your solicitor. I know all about it and want nothing to do with it.'

I received a nasty letter in due course from the solicitor accusing me of not doing my duty. I replied in kind, telling him he knew nothing about the law but that he had every right, under civil law, if he wanted to sue a priest, to go ahead and do it; although, if he did, he was on his own since I was having nothing to do with it.

He also sent a letter to Father McKeever, demanding payment for the dogs he had shot. The good priest read the letter aloud from the pulpit during mass, making great ceremony of dramatically tearing it to pieces on the altar while muttering darkly about "Communists".

The dispute carried on for another fifteen months or so, until eventually another meeting was called within the harrier club the outcome of which was a decision to drop the matter. I bumped into Paddy two days later, 'So, I've heard you've decided against pursuing the case. Perhaps you should have just listened to my advice in the first place. How much do you owe the solicitor?'

Paddy hung his head, 'Two hundred and seventy-five pounds.' I hadn't the heart to admonish him further.

1961: Domestic problems in Ballon

After six happy years in Kilbrittain I decided it was time to make a move. The truth was that by this time, I had been qualified to move to the rank of

Inspector, but there was no room for a promotion in the Kilbrittain station. Indeed, a vacancy had come up but the quota for applicants had been filled by three colleagues who were all personal friends of the Chief. As I was ever anxious to proceed onwards and upwards in my career I felt my only option was to apply for a transfer.

A short while after making my application I was informed that I would be moving to Ballon Garda Station in Carlow. Myself, Nancy and the children packed up and said goodbye to all our good friends, promising to stay in touch.

Perhaps Nancy wished we had stayed in West Cork on seeing the house that was allocated to us in the married quarters of Ballon. It was in an appalling condition. John's reaction spoke for us all when he looked around and cried, 'Oh, Daddy, why did you bring us here. It's awful!' Many an hour was spent scrubbing and dusting until it felt something like home. Cooking and heat was supplied by the big old range in the kitchen, or, at least, that was the plan. In fact the range refused to cooperate. Anytime I lit it, the kitchen disappeared beneath a cloud of black smoke. In a futile attempt to combat the effects of the relentlessly bellowing smoke, I went through six packs of steel wool trying to find the original layer of the kitchen wall underneath the years of grime.

After making enquiries I was given the phone number of the architect who serviced the stations. I rang his Arklow office and introduced myself, explained my situation and asked him for a new range. Unfortunately he was not the most affable of individuals and was rather affronted by my request, refusing outright to accommodate it, 'That range is only three years old so you're not entitled to a new one!' Somewhat surprised at his harsh attitude, I protested that the oven would not heat up and, consequently, my young family were not able to have any proper meals. Finally he agreed that he would come to Ballon to inspect the range in person. Obviously he felt I could not be trusted which – in fairness to him – was true as the oven did actually work but for the amount of smoke that tunnelled out of it, it wasn't worth the effort of lighting it. He told me not to light the fire as he needed do it himself in order to locate the problem. It wasn't the response I was hoping for but what could I say?

He and his assistant arrived early on the Friday. Making their acquaintance with the range, he lit the fire and then sat down at *my* kitchen table, taking up *my* newspaper to read. The oven did nothing out of the ordinary and I could swear to hearing mutterings something along the lines that there was nothing wrong with it and that it was probably the coal I was using. This was not shaping up too well. I wanted a new range and I am a man who is used to getting whatever I have set my sights on!

Thinking fast I told him that perhaps he and his colleague would be so kind as to wait outside in his car as my wife was trying to do her housework and they were proving to be an obstacle. They could come in at intervals to inspect the range's performance. Thankfully they agreed to this. As soon as they went outside I opened up both the damper and the oven door on the range thus allowing the heat to go careering up the chimney. From the station's reception desk, next door, I could see the men in the car and when they opened their doors I ran in to close the damper and door before dashing back to the desk; a perfect picture of innocence. They scratched their heads and went back out to the car, permitting me to open the damper and oven door again for their next visit. This went on for a while until the architect finally came into the station to tell me the unexpected news, 'That's not heating up, Sergeant.' I nodded in weary anticipation. He asked, 'Why isn't it heating up though?' I shrugged, 'I don't know. You're the expert in these matters.'

A short while later a new range was delivered to our house.

1961: Carlow

Four months after taking the job in Ballon a vacancy came up at the station in Carlow town, when the station's sergeant died suddenly from a heart attack. I did not bother to apply for it myself as I knew that eight local officers had put themselves forward for the interview so it seemed rather pointless to add my name, as a recent blow-in, to the list. However I received a phone call from my Chief Superintendent asking why I had not applied for the job. I explained that I didn't want to be presumptuous. 'But, wouldn't you like the station because it's yours if you do.'

'Well, yes, Sir, I would be delighted to have it.'

I could hardly believe when he replied 'It's yours, then!'

I was one of two Sergeants attached to Carlow station, there was the Sergeant in charge of the station, who did all the administrative work while I was the Duty Sergeant, my responsibilities including traffic management and the solving of crime, in short any activities that took place outside the station. Between the two of us, we supervised a staff of twenty-one guards.

The family were delighted to move to Carlow. Since it was only fifty miles from Dublin it meant that Nancy could visit her family much more regularly. I'm afraid to say, however, the conditions in the "married quarters" were once again, appalling. The bathroom was in dire shape while damp had attacked the timber furnishings in the kitchen rendering them completely resistant to any attempt to paint them.

I rang the architect in Arklow and explained that my accommodation was in urgent need of a refurbishment. He was his usual grumpy self and asked for my name. Upon hearing it, he asked, 'Weren't you in Ballon?' I confirmed I was. 'And how long have you been in Carlow?' I told him we had just arrived the previous day. He was indignant, 'You're not there two days and you're complaining already? Well, you can forget it. That building is not due for a refurbishment for another three years. Good day to you!' He put down the phone on me, leaving me wishing I was there with him in Arklow so I could ring his bloody neck!

Luckily enough, a few days later we had a visitor to the station. Mr Carroll was the Commissioner of The Offices of Public Works. He was on a tour of the stations throughout the Carlow and Kildare districts, having left Dublin early that morning. We got into conversation and he told me that he had stopped in Naas to have his sandwich and flask of tea. I was surprised that a man on his salary wasn't having his lunch in a fancy hotel. I told him about the state of the married quarters and he checked his file to confirm that the architect was right about no refurbishment being due for another three years. Seeing a perfect opportunity, I asked him would he care for a cup of tea and bite to eat. After all, they say a way to a man's heart is through his stomach. He readily agreed so I brought him into our dilapidated home to give him his tea. Nancy was in town so I gave John money and sent him off to the local shop to buy lettuce, tomatoes, a tin of salmon and a cake. I put the Commissioner sitting down at the kitchen table but not before apologising for the ugliness and dinginess of his surroundings in which he was about to dine.

As soon as I heard Nancy at the front door I ran out to meet her, urging her to tell Mr Carroll that she couldn't live with the conditions as they were. Nancy refused to complain to him, however, as it just wasn't in her nature. In any case Mr Carroll had already agreed that the place was in a dreadful state and wasn't fit for Nancy and our three young children. He asked me who performed the decorating and construction work for Carlow but I couldn't tell him since I was new to the area. Leaving him chatting to Nancy I went into the station and found out that it was Mr Carberry who had just been seen across the street going into the butchers. I went over and asked him to come to my house, where I introduced him to Mr Carroll who ordered an immediate refurbishment including a brand new bathroom. Nancy and I were delighted. Before he left, he asked me to ring the architect in Arklow and tell him that he personally authorised a refurbishment of our quarters. I smiled to myself, 'Certainly, Sir, and thank you for being so understanding of our situation!' I was certainly looking forward to making that phone call.

After Mr Carroll's visit I went into the station and made the phone call. When I reintroduced myself as Sergeant Bohan to the architect, he snapped, 'I don't want to talk to you!' Suppressing a strong urge to laugh I said as politely as I could manage, 'Please, I'm just passing on a message. Mr Carroll, your boss, wants you to know that he has ordered a full refurbishment of the married quarters here.' The line was silent. Emboldened by the fact that I had won this second battle between us, I fibbed, 'Also, he has specifically asked me to tell you that he wants you here in person to supervise the project.' There was a tense pause before the architect articulated a brief but heartfelt reply, 'You f**k off!' and then he hung up on me a second time. He never turned up but shortly afterwards, our home was completely overhauled with a new bathroom, new furniture and coats of fresh paint everywhere.

There was a great variety of ages, backgrounds and experience among the guards based in the station. Seven of them were senior and had worked in Carlow town since the station was established in 1922. By now I knew that having a good local knowledge of one's district was fifty per cent of good police work, and was highly appreciative of the experience of these men. On the other hand the twelve younger guards were highly enthusiastic about their job. I felt I had the best of both worlds and in the combination of the keen ambitions of the younger members with the experience and wisdom of those who were older, I truly believed we could do a good job in upholding the law.

I like to think that I always treated my staff with respect. If a guard made a mistake through incompetence while trying to do his best I would never say anything to him. This was my general attitude: all you can expect is their best however incompetent that is.

I took to visiting the County Home for Waifs and Strays on a regular basis, getting to know the temporary lodgers. They proved to be a great source of information and, more often than not, were able to help me out with crimes that had been committed around Carlow as well as the outer districts. In due course I was able to pass on important and highly relevant information to other garda stations. With the incentive of a few cigarettes the "knights of the road" made my visits more than worthwhile with the amount of sometimes seemingly incidental information they would divulge to me which would subsequently turn out to be invaluable.

One night Peter O'Rourke called into the station to tell me that the nun on the door of the home was refusing to let him inside on account of the fact that he had been quite drunk on his last stay. I couldn't believe it. It was an absolutely freezing cold night, the sort of night you wouldn't leave a dog outside. I got my coat and we walked over to the home.

The Sister wasn't swayed by my presence and told me in no uncertain terms that she was not letting Peter in. 'But, Sister', I argued, 'If you don't let him in he's going to have to sleep rough.' She sniffed, 'Well, he should have thought of that before.' I looked at her in amazement and then was obliged to pull rank on her, so to speak, 'Well, Sister, all I can say is that it is a dangerously cold night. If you condemn this man to sleep in the street you could be condemning him to death. And let me tell you if that happens, I will be forced to give evidence that you were the reason he met his death.' She still held fast on the door, thinking about this. I added in my most exasperated tone, 'Really, Sister, do you want this on your conscience? Where is your Christian charity?' Finally she saw sense and opened the door to let Peter in, ungraciously snapping at him, 'Oh, very well, get in but I'm warning you to behave yourself!' I wished them both a good night and returned to the station, wondering why it was that the local Sergeant had seen it necessary to get involved in trying to enlighten a nun as to the real meaning of charity.

***

It was the summer of 1961 and a stray Alsatian dog had made its way, from wherever it originated, into Carlow Town. Following a number of complaints about it snarling at adults and children alike, my colleague, Sergeant Quinlan, came to the noble conclusion, 'You should do something about that bloody Alsatian!' I left the station and made a few enquiries before finding the dog fast asleep on Tullow Street, outside Hatton's Drapery shop. I needed a few minutes to consider my options and came up with a bit of a brainwave, even if I say so myself!

I went into Michael White's chemist and asked him for something that would quickly put the dog into a deep sleep. Sleep, mind, I don't mean I was looking to poison it. Michael reached into one of his presses and handed me a packet containing some powder, 'There, you go! That would knock out a horse in ten minutes'. I thanked him, took the prescription and headed across the street to the butchers, where I asked for a piece of liver. Next I mashed the powder into the meat and headed back across to the drapery shop where the dog was now awake and watching me curiously through half-open eyes. Approaching him as carefully as I could, I dropped the liver at his feet and was relieved to see him gobble it right up. 'Good boy!' I exclaimed and returned to the station to fetch my strawberry net.

You see, it was not a very elaborate plan. It was simple and practical and, therefore, I was fully confident in its able execution. The dog would fall asleep, thereby easily allowing me to catch it in my net with injury to neither man nor beast. My colleagues complimented me on its conception while Tom Walsh, the driver of our patrol car, offered his assistance which I readily accepted. Net in hand, we drove to Tulles Street where I was relieved to see the dog was still fast asleep. My plan was going perfectly. Stepping out of the car I walked boldly up to him and dropped my strawberry net over his sleeping form. He woke up immediately, startling me and Tom both, jumped to his feet and promptly set about ripping my net to shreds in a matter of seconds.

Sounding a temporary retreat Tom drove me back to the station where I explained the situation to Sergeant Quinlan. 'I know what will solve the problem', he said. 'We'll go up to the sugar factory and get one of their great big nets. That will definitely hold him.' This we did, this time with Sergeant Quinlan joining our posse so as to ensure that this time the dog would surely be captured. The net they handed over to us at the sugar factory was in fact, so big that we couldn't close the boot on it. Our next stop was back on Tullow Street but by now the dog was nowhere to be seen. We drove around the town in search of him and finally found him asleep in the yard of the Royal Hotel, in Dublin Street.

It was about eleven o'clock in the morning and there was a wedding breakfast in full swing. In those days weddings began with a nine o'clock mass followed by a meal immediately afterwards. My esteemed colleagues and I walked into the yard and took care to lock the gate behind us, thus preventing the dog's possible escape. Through the dining room windows, the wedding party could see three uniformed guards holding aloft a huge net and were understandably curious, more so when I, to cause a bit of excitement, began to look upwards in an expectant manner. The guests naturally concluded that we were preparing to catch whichever poor soul was planning to jump from the roof of the hotel. Some of them came to the front door to watch the proceedings and understandably did not appear too disappointed to find out that they had got it wrong.

We continued our approach; I was to the right of Sergeant Quinlan while Tom was to his left. When we were about fifteen yards from the dog he opened his eyes, jumped up and, as we had cornered him, made a run for the centre of the net. Tom and I instinctively moved towards one another, successfully enveloping the animal in the net – albeit with the good Sergeant! The dog snapped at him in fright, which was wholly understandable, while the entangled Sergeant lit up the place with raging curses, much to the pleasure of the tipsy onlookers who generously cheered and applauded the entire performance.

Eventually we got him released – the Sergeant – but held the dog in safe custody. I put a lead on him – the dog – and led him back to the station. He was quite docile after his stressful experience and meekly ate the food I put in front of him.

The following day I took a phone call from a lady in Leighlinbridge who had heard about the unwanted Alsatian and offered to take him off our hands. Some weeks later I bumped into her and asked after her new pet, 'Ah, he's a delight, Sergeant Bohan, such a lovely, quiet animal!'

'Well', I replied, 'Tell him Sergeant Quinlan was asking after him.'

***

There was an old council store in town from which eighteen black copper boilers had been stolen. I went down to inspect the scene and found that the culprit had gained access through the window which was almost covered by ivy. There was no hint as to the robber's identity until I had the good fortune to think of pulling back the ivy from the window and was duly rewarded with the sight of a distinctive thumbprint on the glass.

A short while later I found out that the boilers had been sold to a dealer in Kilkenny so I made my way there to meet him and get a description of the seller. The fingerprint was identified as belonging to a traveller, Michael McCawley, of no fixed abode. The search was on.

I made a point of keeping in touch with the hotels in Carlow, the Royal and the Crofton. Hotels can prove to be a wonderful source of information. The receptionist from the Crofton rang me to say that they had a resident who was very well-dressed and had booked a room for a couple of days. However, when house-keeping went in to clean the room they found that the man had not slept in his bed, instead he had spread straw over the floor beside the bed and slept there. She described the man and I knew it was Mr McCawley. I told her to ring me as soon as he returned to the hotel.

True to her word she rang me later to say he had arrived back at the hotel. I went over and, following a brief interrogation, he confessed to the theft. I'll always remember that case since it was surely unique in that the culprit was apprehended due to his singular preference for straw on the floor as opposed to a comfortable hotel bed! It's strange how sometimes, our most personal predilections betray us!

***

I remember a particularly sad case in Carlow. Months of heavy rain had caused the River Barrow to flood. Tragedy struck when a four year old boy, on his way home from school, wanted to test his brand new wellington boots and walked into the water. The strong current immediately seized him and swept him away. We quickly organised a search and had the river dragged several times but could not find him. I felt that his slight frame would have immediately been taken down the river and, to prove this, I put stones and straw into a sack, making it equal to the boy's approximate weight and threw it in the water. I stood and watched as the sack was immediately taken down the river and out of sight.

A few days later I organised another big search and was moved by the huge number of volunteers who turned up to help us. However, the search took a frightening turn when three young men, who went out on the river in their own boat ended up toppling into the water, such was the strength of the current. I felt I had no option but to call off the search because I couldn't risk having a second tragedy on my hands. We spent the next two months looking for the young boy in vain.

His distressed father refused to give up hope and walked the banks of the river every single day for six long months until the little body was finally found, caught up in the mill's wheel at Milford. The funeral was the biggest I had ever seen. People came from miles around to show their support for the boy's family. It was extremely moving. His mother and father spoke about being privileged to have been the parents of an angel.

Shortly after I arrived in Carlow a vacancy came up for Inspector. I had only been a Sergeant for a relatively short period of time and reckoned it was too early for me to progress to that rank. Moreover, there were plenty of others applying for the position, and they were a lot more senior to me. In the end a Sergeant from Newbridge got the job. Of course, this meant that there was now a vacancy for a Sergeant in Newbridge. I wasn't interested in the position there since my family had been through many changes and moves in the previous few years and Nancy and I were eager to settle in Carlow for the foreseeable future.

My Superintendent was called to attend a conference with the Chief Superintendent and other superintendents to discuss the vacancies and promotions. On his return he told me that when the Chief was asked who he was sending to Newbridge to fill the vacant position he replied, 'Sergeant Bohan from Carlow.' When I heard this I told my Superintendent that it was too much. I had worked at two different stations in the last couple of years, uprooting the children from three schools, (in Kilbrittain, Ballon and Carlow) and newfound friends. He asked me what I was going to do and I assured him that I wanted to appeal the decision. So he rang the Chief Superintendent to tell him that I did not want to take the position in Newbridge, resulting in the Chief asking me to meet him at his office in Naas. My appointment was made for half-past ten the following Monday morning.

I turned up at the specified time in uniform and was bid to wait outside in the Public Office until the Chief was ready for me. After a few minutes I was told I could go in. I found him seated behind his desk, paperwork piled high in front of him. 'Well, Sergeant', he asked, 'What is the purpose of your visit?' His question threw me as he had been the one to summon me to meet him. I outlined my problem, explaining that I didn't want to have to take the children out of school and, furthermore, my wife was upset at the thought of having to move so soon again.

There was also a further complication in the fact that I could not afford the rent of a house in Newbridge, where the average rent was two pounds and fifty shillings, a huge increase on my present rent of one pound. He listened politely but didn't seem overly sympathetic. 'Sergeant, Newbridge is the most important station in my division. Therefore, it would be a good career move and I'd make sure that you would be the number one Sergeant. In other words, if you took this job you would be next in line for a promotion. And if you don't take it, you'll have to live with the consequences.' Unsure what he meant by that, I offered, 'But I have a good record.' He sighed, 'Look, go home and discuss it with your wife.'

'But, Sir', I said, 'I already have. She doesn't want to move.' He began to get irritated and dismissed me by saying, 'Just go away and talk it over with your wife again and ring me at four o'clock.' There was nothing for it but to leave, promising him that I'd ring him later. I didn't bother trying to change Nancy's mind since mine was already made up. When I got back to Carlow I rang him but he was busy so I left a message saying that nothing had changed and I didn't want the transfer. He never rang me back.

I had heard that the Chief Superintendent actually liked and respected me well enough but he did hold one thing against me and that was my refusal to go to Newbridge. I experienced a little of this when, a few months later, he arrived at my station to make an inspection. He arranged to come at six o'clock in the evening which was an unusual time for a visit. As usual the men were examined on their knowledge of various acts and procedures. We had decided on the examination topic in advance of his visit. He also asked them for their knowledge of well-known criminals in the Carlow district and adjoining division, looking for names, physical descriptions and lists of offences. All of this information was in the *Fogra Tora* magazine, the Garda's information booklet.

They provided him with the right answers but then he surprised us all by asking for one criminal's "Fogra" number. Criminals were listed by number in the book but that number had nothing to do with any paperwork that would have to be filled in after an arrest. In other words it was a completely unnecessary question that should not have been part of the inspection. As it happened, one of my officers had written a few notes on his hands and, for some reason, had written down this criminal's Fogra number. I saw him take a quick look at the palm of his right hand and then give the number to the Chief. However, I was unprepared to let the Chief away with this and said, 'Chief, with all respect, I think that's an unfair question. When we arrest this man he won't have that number branded across his forehead.' To my relief, he nodded and said, 'Quite so, Sergeant. That will do for the inspection.' I firmly believe that I made the right decision to pull him up on the unfair question because I firmly believe that a Sergeant had to be loyal to his staff. And, by the by, we did arrest that particular individual a few weeks after the Chief's visit but not with any reference to his Fogra Tora number!

That summer there was a big carnival in Carlow town. People came from all over and, in a single afternoon, quite a number of cars that were parked in the centre of the town had been broken into. Coats, hats and even, on one occasion, knitting wool were amongst the various items which had caught the eye of the thieves. A report was received that four spare tyres for a Ford Anglia car had been stolen from four different cars. In those days there were serial numbers on tyres. In respect of three of the tyres the owners were able to provide us with receipts which had the serial numbers printed on them.

One morning, one of the younger guards, Bill Hynes, came into work and asked me, 'Do you know who I just saw in town, driving an old banger of a Ford Anglia, Peter Smith's son, Joe. Do you think there's any chance he's our man?' It was definitely worth looking into. Joe was a bit of a ne'er do well who had never worked a day in his life.

Bill and I paid a visit to the Smith's house where we spoke to Joe's mother who told us that her son was elsewhere following up on a driving job. I didn't want to show my hand since we had absolutely no evidence yet that her son was the culprit. What we needed was to get a close up of the tyres on his car. Thinking fast, I asked her if he could drive a pick-up truck. 'Oh, of course he could!' she said. 'Well, I believe the manager at the sugar factory is in need of a driver to make deliveries; can you send him to see me as soon as he gets back and I'll have a word with him?'

A little while after I returned to the station Joe arrived asking to speak with me. Small talk with the guard on the desk had let us know that he had parked his car outside. I gave the nod; Joe came to my office while the guard went out to check his Ford Anglia. Sure enough my phone rang a couple of minutes later, 'Sergeant, you have the bird with you. Two of his tyres carry the missing serial numbers.'

Unfortunately for Joe, the interview for the job turned into an interview of a very different sort, with no possibility of denying the charges nor indeed of securing paid employment! He brought us back to his house where we found all the missing items in a plastic bag that was concealed beneath a sheet of corrugated iron in the nearby ditch. Much to his mother's annoyance we arrested him and charged him under the Larceny Act of 1916. He was released on bail to appear at Carlow District Court two weeks later. There, he pleaded guilty to all the charges and was sentenced to twelve months imprisonment, suspended on the condition that he entered into a bond to keep the peace and be of good behaviour, which he duly did. I must say that there was always a great sense of satisfaction when following the detection of a crime, I was able to return stolen goods to their rightful owners.

***

One of the more interesting cases I worked on in Carlow involved fraudulent cheques. The manager of Lipton's Shop had lodged a cheque for ninety pounds with the Munster and Leinster Bank. The cheque was returned to him a few days later as being fraudulent. He explained that the cheque was given to him by one Joe Arnold who was a valued customer of the shop for twenty-five years. Joe had presented the cheque in Lipton's, the cheque being made payable to him and signed by a J. Ryan. Every Saturday Joe Arnold would arrive to do his weekly shopping. The story went that on one particular Saturday Joe was waiting by the side of the road in the hope a neighbour was driving to town and could give him a lift. A red ford lorry stopped and the driver offered to bring him to town. When Joe explained he was heading to do his shopping in Lipton's, the driver gave him a cheque with a shopping list of his own, saying, 'I'd be much obliged if you could get this for me. Leave it in Kirwan's shop and I can collect it later. And sure if you're around I can bring you and your shopping home too.' They agreed on a time to meet since Joe had other things to do about the town but when he walked to Kirwan's the driver had already been and gone with the shopping.

A second cheque – for eighty pounds – bounced, this time in Kelly's drapery shop in Castlecomer, in Kilkenny. Again it had been made payable to Joe Arnold and was signed by J. Ryan. The customer was a grey-haired, middle aged woman who had used the bad cheque to buy an umbrella, two good blankets and a gabardine coat. The serial number was one up from the Lipton cheque so I asked the bank manager who the cheque book had been issued to. He told me it was issued to Mr Butler, a local farmer and bachelor who mostly kept himself to himself. When I spoke with the cashier and asked who had collected the cheque book I was surprised that he couldn't remember if Mr Butler had actually collected it himself or it had been given out to someone else to be delivered to him.

The following day I visited Joe Arnold's house with another guard. It was a very dilapidated place in dire need of repair and renovation. We found it a little peculiar that he never invited us inside; instead he came out and sat in our car. Perhaps he was ashamed of his home. A man in his sixties, he seemed quite upset to be mixed up in such an unpleasant situation. I asked him to describe the red lorry and its driver for me; he said it was loaded up with grain and that the driver was about my height, with dark hair, wearing overalls and wellington boots, the tops of which were turned down. He also said that there was a lady in the cab of the truck who, as they veered around a sharp corner, had shouted out, 'be careful, John!' So, now we had a name as well as a description.

My colleague and I toured the various mills in the area to ask about a red lorry driven by a man called John but nobody admitted to accepting such a load of grain over the last few days. However, we did hear about a man from Kerry who drove a red lorry and had recently returned from working in England. I went to see him but he did not fit the physical description in the least and his lorry wasn't a Ford. The man we were looking for was still at large so I put extra guards out on the road to look out for a red lorry driven by a man with dark hair who answered to the name of John. Both he and his vehicle seemed to have disappeared into thin air as the results remained at zero sightings.

For the want of something to do I decided to pay another visit to Joe Arnold with Garda Tom Walsh. Once again he came out of his house to sit in the car with us. I asked him for another description of the driver as I simply couldn't understand how we had not found this man who was presumably local. Joe was very understanding and happy to be of assistance to the Gardaí. He repeated what he remembered about the man, that he was about six foot, dark haired, wearing overalls but now he was rather pleased to be able to furnish a detail he had forgotten about earlier, he told me that the lace on the man's left shoe was untied. I thanked him for his time and watched him walk back inside his house.

'Tom', I said, 'We have our man.' Tom looked at me in surprise, 'How so?' 'Were you listening to the description of the driver, the first time he was wearing wellington boots and now his shoe lace is untied.' Tom laughed and said, 'Ah, yes!' I told him to report for duty at eight o'clock, the following morning, by which time I would have acquired a search warrant.

We drove back out to the house the next morning. As usual Joe came out to the car to see what we wanted. I said to him, 'I think we have the culprit, Joe, but I need your help to identify him.' The expression on Joe's face was quite a picture. Nevertheless he made a big fuss about getting into the car, believing he was on his way to the station to confirm that we had arrested the driver of the red Ford truck. He sat in the back seat expectantly, wondering why Tom didn't start the engine and drive us off towards the station. Maybe half a minute passed before he ventured to ask, 'Are we not moving?' This was my cue, 'No, Joe, we are not and I'll tell you why, we know you're the culprit.' Joe folded immediately, 'Ah Jesus Christ! It's not my fault. Honest to God, the bloody bitch made me do it!'

Finally we got inside his house. I found the cheque book under the mattress before finding the umbrella, blankets and gabardine coat in the wardrobe. When I took out the items Mrs Arnold started screaming and then ran out the back door. We didn't see her for two days. To this day I don't know where she spent her time in hiding. However, when she did finally emerge, she was of course arrested immediately.

The cheque book had been ordered from the bank in Mr Butler's name and had been collected by them, as a "favour" to their neighbour, who was completely unaware of its existence. J Ryan was the cattle dealer John

Ryan, and his name was used to explain the large amounts of the cheques. When Joe was asked why he had such a large cheque he said that he had just sold cattle to John Ryan. In fact he had sold cattle to John a while back who had paid him with a cheque thus giving Mrs Arnold the idea of stealing a cheque book. The red lorry and the driver were completely fictional creations; Joe had fed us that story simply as a way of throwing us off the scent, in vain, as it transpired.

The Arnolds were a respectable couple in the community, or – at least – appeared to be so. As the Manager had said, they had been valued customers of Liptons for the previous twenty-five years.

They were both sentenced to six months imprisonment but the sentence was suspended on condition that they both enter into a bond, to the sum of a hundred pounds, to behave themselves and keep the peace for the next three years, which they did. I felt they had learned their lesson and would be retiring from their temporary brush with a life of crime.

1962 Cavan

Following a tough interview I was promoted to the rank of Inspector on 19 January 1962 and informed that I was being posted to Cavan. I was pretty pleased with this as it meant I was only thirty miles from Leitrim and could visit my mother a lot more easily.

Upon arriving in Cavan, in February 1962, I secured rented accommodation in the form of a bungalow that sat about a mile from the town, at the entrance to St Patrick's College. The rent, at three pounds a week, was very reasonable and my landlord was no less than the Bishop of Kilmore. The rooms were small but in good condition, a pleasant improvement on some of the places we had rented in the past. The only problem was that, owing to the amount of trees that surrounded the house, we were unable to receive any television channels, much to the disappointment of the children!

The station, which was also district headquarters, was in the town centre and staffed by two sergeants, twenty guards and the

Superintendent.

One afternoon I received a phone call from Mr Anderson, who was the headmaster of the girls' grammar school. He told me that two of his pupils had gone into town at lunch-time. I was horrified to hear that one of the girls had been pulled into a car, right in front of her friend who had immediately raced back to school to raise the alarm. The only information we had was that the car had a northern registration plate. There was no time to lose.

Tim Mulvey, the station's driver, and I jumped into our patrol car and took off in search of the kidnapper. After a quick tour of the town we drove out, heading for the north, when we spied a young girl stumbling along the side of the road. She was in tears. We pulled over immediately and she identified herself as the missing student, saying that she had just been attacked. In spite of her distress she was still able to provide us with a good description of the driver. I brought her to the nearest house, leaving her in the care of a kindly lady and rang the station to send a car for her, telling them that she needed to be medically examined.

Tim and I took off at great speed for the border. Thanks to Tim we caught up with the culprit at Ballyconnell, County Cavan. We turned on our siren and Tim flashed his lights, indicating that we wanted to pass him by but he never slowed down. A few more miles and we would reach the border, separating the North of Ireland from the Republic. Tom agonised at the wheel, 'We can't go much further! We won't be able to catch him once he's into the six counties and Enniskillen is only just up the road.'

There was no way I was letting this man escape. 'Alright, Tim. We'll change places. I'll drive and I'll take full responsibility if we have to cross the Border. The bastard is not going to get away!'

We finally caught him just beyond the Slipper Ballroom, (which was outside my jurisdiction), thanks to a farmer driving his cattle on the road, thereby preventing the culprit from overtaking him. I drove up behind him, was able to overtake him and force him to come to a stop. There was little conversation. I got him out of his car and put him in the back of ours and we drove him straight back to Cavan where I interviewed him. He admitted to snatching the girl and assaulting her. He told me that he had intended to rape her but then lost his nerve. We kept him overnight and he was in the local court the very next day. I can't remember who his solicitor was but he must have been a very good one as he was sentenced to a mere six months for the attack. It wasn't nearly enough. Plus he was eventually released from prison having served just four months of his sentence.

However he was never seen in Cavan again so that was something of a good result, though I often wondered if he had moved elsewhere to continue his life of crime.

1963: Ulster Football Final

My Superintendent was on his summer holidays so I was in charge. The big match was coming up on 28 July, with Donegal taking on Down in Cavan's GAA stadium, Breffni Park in the final of the Ulster championship. It promised to be a great day. My job was to ensure that everything ran smoothly, including the traffic which would take some preparation, given the size of the crowd that was expected.

On the day itself I had two tractors at pivotal points either side of the town. They were there to tow away any cars that got stuck or broke down or were parked illegally, blocking the flow of traffic. I had a Garda on a motorbike patrolling the Dublin/Cavan Road. Everyone had strict instructions to contact me by radio if anything untoward happened. Unfortunately my Garda motorcyclist went for his dinner without bothering to notify me or anyone else. As a result, one of the busiest roads was left unsupervised and a car had been "parked" or more correctly abandoned, in most unintelligent fashion by a driver who was either very stupid or very selfish, depending on your point of view. It wasn't long before the obstruction it was causing began to cause major traffic problems.

A bus, that was forced to move on the inside of the car in an attempt to pass it, ended up leaving the road completely, finishing up in the ditch. As you can imagine, the traffic came to a complete standstill. When I came on the scene I had no option but to break a window of the car so that I could get in and move it out of the way. I left a note for the driver to contact me. He was probably lucky that he never did as I would have given him a right earful of abuse.

Since I didn't have a sufficient number of guards to police the event, the GAA hired twenty Gardaí from the adjoining Granard District to perform the duties which were of a non-police nature and it would be the club that would be paying their wages for the day.

Just after the match started, Hughie Riley, the County Secretary of Cavan's GAA, came looking for me. He told me that there were about twenty people sitting on the roof of the ticket office and he feared that the entire building was likely to collapse under their weight. But that wasn't the reason he was so upset. It turned out that one of the people on the roof was one of the guards he had hired from Granard. Hughie asked the Garda to please get down but the man had blatantly and rudely refused to budge.

I went down to the ticket office myself and ordered the man off the roof. He immediately complied and we got everyone else down too. However Hughie was so upset over the guard's rudeness that he told me he would not be paying the wages of any of the twenty Gardaí from the Granard Station. I certainly didn't have the budget to cover any extra salaries and, besides, I felt that Hughie was over excited. He was a good man at heart but he did feel that he had been poorly treated. 'Hughie, there was only one Garda on the roof. It wouldn't be right to punish the other nineteen who were performing their duties as you wanted them to.' It only took him a couple of seconds to give in, 'Okay, I'll pay nineteen wages but no more!' This did not suit me either; I would hate to see a man lose a day's pay for a stupid mistake. I told Hughie to come and see me at my office the next morning; I felt that I could smooth things over if he had a day to calm himself down.

Accordingly, I had my story ready for Hughie when he arrived bang on time the following day. I plied him with tea and biscuits as he told me there was no way he was paying for the rude guard. Pretending to nod in agreement, I sighed, 'His poor wife...though it's probably for the best in the long run.' This stopped Hughie in his tracks and he asked me to explain what I meant. 'Oh', I said, 'It's just... well...the sad truth is that the man is a complete alcoholic. His wife doesn't know what to do. They have a big family and with this latest escapade he'll probably lose his job now. It will be one complaint too many.' Hughie shook his head, 'No way, I can't have that! I'll not be the reason that a man loses his job. I'll pay his wages and we'll say no more about it.'

My little problem was solved and I was genuine in my thanks to Hughie for his kindness, although I had lied to him about the guard being both an alcoholic and married. However, you may be sure that I gave the guard a stern dressing down for making such a poor showing of An Garda Síochána.

And for anyone who is interested, the match ended with the score Down 2–11 to Donegal 1–04.

***

In August 1963 Nancy gave birth to our second son, whom we named Michael. About six months later John was due to make his Confirmation. When he came down with a very bad flu Nancy suggested that we call the doctor. A short while later, the Doctor arrived out to the house, had a look at John and prescribed him with medicine, assuring us that he should be fit and well and able to make his confirmation.

I walked the doctor out to his car where he surprised me by saying that he was concerned about the baby. 'Why? What's wrong?' He looked at me and said, 'I think he's sub-normal.' Yes, it is an awful word but you have to remember it was over forty years ago. He got into his car and drove off. I stayed outside the house crying. When I managed to recover myself I went back in. Nancy asked me out straight, 'Did he say anything about Michael?' I was amazed. When I repeated his words she admitted that she had suspected something was wrong since the day after his birth but had hoped and prayed that she was mistaken.

We arranged to have Michael properly assessed by a psychologist who diagnosed him as having Down's Syndrome. In those days there was no help available for the family, with no one to talk to or advise us as to what the future was going to hold for our son. We simply brought him home and loved him just as much as we loved our other children. Today, I am pleased to report that Michael has grown into a loving, charming, witty and happy go-lucky man who leads a fulfilled life and is much loved by his family as well as all of those who help to take care of him.

1964: Murder in Cavan

One Saturday night a report came in that a patient had escaped from the mental hospital in Monaghan. He had been missing since three o'clock in the afternoon. His family, wife, daughter and mother-in-law, lived in Cullis which was two miles from Cavan Town. In other words this was where we were going to look for him before trying anywhere else.

Garda Tim Mulvey accompanied me to the house. As we drove up the lane towards the house, we met the escapee. He was on foot, covered in blood, completely distraught and appeared unable to answer any of the questions we put to him. We brought him to the Garda station in Cavan and then rushed back to Cullis to check on the family. Our worst fears were confirmed when we found the man's wife lying on her back with a severe wound to her head, a rock beside her which was covered in blood. There was no sign of her daughter or mother. The poor woman never regained consciousness and died the following afternoon.

I have never felt as sorry for anyone as I did for that man. I took a statement from him and readily believed that had I asked him if he had recently visited the moon he would have told me that he had. It was hard to accept that he had no notion at all of what he had done – to bludgeon his wife to death and not to know a thing about it. I'll never forget the look in his eyes, and can only describe it as deranged. We took samples of blood from his clothes and kept him in a cell overnight. We also took samples of blood from the wife's body and also from her bloodied clothes.

When we returned to the house the next day we found the distressed daughter and grandmother. They had fled the house in their bare feet, hiding out in a nearby field.

The preliminary hearing was held in Cavan District Court where a thorough medical examination was called for, to determine if the husband was fit to plead. The examination determined that he was not; he was certified as being criminally insane and was sent to Dundrum mental hospital for indefinite detention.

1964: Castlereagh, County Roscommon

Having served in Cavan for almost two years, I was interviewed for the position of Superintendent. The interview board consisted of three senior members of An Garda Síochána. Firstly, Commissioner Dan Costigan who was, in my opinion, one of the best commissioners we ever had. A breath of fresh air in the force, he did away with all of the draconian regulations. For example, there were rules that stipulated that you couldn't leave your sub-district or wear plain clothes without the permission of the Superintendent. Also, small police stations played host to ridiculous shifts. If you were performing the role of "Station Orderly", which meant that you were on the reception desk while simultaneously handling any problems that arose, you started work at nine o'clock in the morning, had relief for a half-hour lunch and a half-hour tea break and you then worked straight through until nine o'clock the following morning. Imagine having to sit at the desk for twenty-four hours knowing that there probably wouldn't be any visitors and just one phone call, the standard test call from the local Post Office at ten o'clock to check that the line was accessible. It was a lamentable waste of time and police resources.

Commissioner Costigan changed all that. The small quiet stations could now close at six in the evening and put a notice in their window displaying the phone number of the District Headquarters where there was a twenty-four hour service available. His approach was one of practicality, shedding the pointless rules that no one else had bothered to question.

The other two interviewers were Deputy Commissioner Flood and Assistant Commissioner Mooney. They interviewed me for about an hour, asking me questions like what I felt I could bring to the position; did I have any suggestions to make that might improve the job; how would I deal with guards who weren't pulling their own weight etc.

I felt that the interview had gone well and this was duly confirmed when I was told that I would be taking up the position of Superintendent at the station in Castlereagh, County Roscommon. I was delighted with this. I had never served in the West of Ireland so this was a wonderful opportunity. The only problem was the issue of accommodation. Nancy and I took a trip over to the town and though we travelled a radius of twenty-five miles from Castlereagh, we could find no suitable rental accommodation.

I rang Sergeant Neary, in the station, explaining I hadn't found anywhere to live and he told me that when any visiting Inspector came out to relieve the Superintendent they stayed with a Miss Agnes Coogan who lived a short distance outside the town. Delighted to hear this, I asked him to contact her and see if she would be willing to give me lodgings until I found a place for the whole family to live. He rang me back the next day with the good news that she had an available room.

My first day in the Castlereagh Station was Monday 15 June. There wasn't much to do aside from some minor correspondence. I finished this by half past two and spent the rest of the day chatting to the District Sergeant. Just before six o'clock I asked him if he would accompany me to Miss Coogan's house to make the expected introductions.

Now, after my years in the force, I had acquired pointers about a person's residence. It had become a rule of mine, that if the curtains on a house were dirty and if there was a brass handle on the front door that looked like it had never known the swipe of a cloth, I knew not to expect the interior to be much better. My stomach sank as Sergeant Neary led me up the path to Miss Coogan's door. Both the curtains and handle were thoroughly grimy though I hid my dismay from my colleague. He knocked on the door which was eventually opened by a woman whose head was adorned with a crown of pink curlers and a hair net, and who had a fag dangling perilously from the side of her downturned mouth. Her apron was covered in ancient grease while the blue veins could be clearly seen on her bare, stubbly legs. What would I have given to be able to walk away with the Sergeant once he made the necessary introductions? The thought did fleetingly pass through my mind that perhaps we could pretend that we had knocked at the wrong house, but too late as my colleague had already greeted my hostess, told her who I was and promptly disappeared, leaving me in the dubious care of Miss Coogan.

She led me inside, into her gloomy front room. It was a glorious summer's evening though you wouldn't have guessed that standing in this room, thanks to the heavy curtain that was pulled all the way across the window. I sat down tentatively wondering about the condition of the multitude of cushions under my rear, which, even in the dim light appeared to be covered in some sort of animal hair. Miss Coogan asked me what I would like for my tea. 'Perhaps a small fry if that's not too much trouble', I answered.

About twenty minutes later my tea arrived on a plate that was emblazoned all around the edge by a series of dirty thumb prints. If I had found such clear, impressive prints at the scene of a crime I would have been half-way to solving it. Doing my best to ignore them I began to eat. My landlady sat down beside me and smoked away, oblivious to my discomfort. When she asked me what I would like for supper I said just a cup of tea with a couple of biscuits. I judged it to be the safest bet.

Even at this early stage in proceedings, I already had decided that I hated the place; however I was stuck there until I could find somewhere else. A couple of evenings later I came home to a dinner of boiled chops. Indeed they looked every bit as unappetising as they sound and it was all I could do to merely push them around the plate unwilling and unable to eat more than a polite half a mouthful. As she watched me she made some sort of apology for her "Uncle Joe". This being the first I had heard of the existence of the said "Uncle Joe", I politely enquired about him and was surprised to learn that she had an elderly and infirmed relative tucked away in a bedroom upstairs. I certainly hadn't heard him making any disturbance and told her as much since she seemed to think he may have bothered me in some way. She then launched into a tirade about how moody and ungrateful he was.

'Oh, yes, he gives me endless trouble. Why, just yesterday I went to the bother of buying and cooking two chops for him. He played with them for ages before finally taking a single bite and ordering me to take them away. I don't know why I bother! Well I tell you I don't waste food like that in this house!'

I wanted to stand up and scream blue bloody murder as reality dawned; the bold Uncle Joe's scorned chops from yesterday had become my dinner for today. I don't remember what happened next, all I know is that I went back to the station that very evening and told Sergeant Neary, 'You have got to help me get out of that place because I'm either going to end up in a mental home or else I'm going to strangle that woman!'

Fortunately he was able to come up with a proposal for my rescue and salvation. He had remembered a Mrs Hoolihan who lived just over the street. She was a widow with a spare room. The Sergeant rang her, explaining that his new Superintendent was interested in taking the room but she refused. Feeling that she was slightly intimidated by my rank and might be thinking I would be demanding and expecting to be fussed over, I decided to go and see her in person. I was delighted to note that her curtains were spotlessly clean and the brass handle shone brightly, allowing me to check my reflection before she opened the door. Well, she was the complete opposite in appearance and personality to the "lovely" Miss Coogan. I explained that I was from Leitrim and so had been brought up on plain and simple food, so if she was able to give me a plate of bacon and cabbage in the evening and clean sheets to sleep in, I would be more than content. To my great relief she agreed to take me in. It made such a difference to not having to dread going "home" after work, wondering what in God's name I'd have to pretend to eat or who had slept in the bed before me. I ended up staying there for three months until I finally found suitable accommodation for my family who I visited at the weekends during the interim.

Castlereagh was a peaceful place to work. The most common offence was a farmer driving his cattle along the road, ignoring the fact that the car behind him might be in a hurry. The crime capital of Ireland it was not.

Indeed the biggest problem I dealt with was to do with a post office dispute in Ballintubber. The postmistress had recently died and it was generally expected that her niece, who had worked alongside her since leaving school, would be appointed to her aunt's job. However, it was not to be. The man who owned the hardware store wanted the contract and he applied and was successful. The locals were far from impressed, feeling that the qualified and experienced niece deserved the job over anyone else.

The village was divided in two, the majority taking the side of the niece of the former post mistress. Feelings were running hot and high with an assembly of locals taking up position outside the post office in protest. It eventually came to the stage where we had to bring in extra protection for the post office. Actually there wouldn't have been a real problem if I had a different Sergeant stationed there. Unfortunately I was stuck with a man who lacked both tact and common sense. His only contribution was to stir the situation, going back and forth between the two sides, telling stories to each one about the other side and generally further igniting the already volatile situation. Accordingly, I found it necessary to visit Ballinatubber every day not just to try to subdue the angry protestors but also to keep the Sergeant in check.

Another guard who worked there was Ned Ryan. He had previously served in Carrick-on-Shannon where he had collected the agricultural statistics. He submitted a claim for subsistence allowance and the travelling expenses he incurred in the collecting of the statistics. When the claim reached my desk I sent it on to the Accounts Branch in the Department of Justice. Two weeks later the claim was returned with a note from the accountant seeking an explanation as to why the Garda visited fewer houses and travelled fewer miles on certain days. I sent the claim back to Ryan for his explanation. However the Sergeant, the trouble-maker, neglected to pass the file to Ned Ryan. Instead he took it upon himself to provide the explanation. He sent his report to me, pointing out that he had served in An Garda Síochána, for nine years, in different stations throughout Leitrim:

> During which time I collected agricultural statistics and census of the population. My heart bleeds for Ned Ryan, for the onerous task he undertook in getting any form of information from Leitrim people. I can say, without fear of contradiction, that they are a dull,

ignorant, non-cooperative and non-cultured race of people.

...that if they are visited by members of An Garda Síochána seeking information that would involve them in the payment of income tax, they can be seen peeping out from behind their curtains in a manner reminiscent of Brinsley MacNamara's book, "The Valley of the Squinting Windows".

I strongly recommend payment of Ned Ryan's claim without further or necessary delay.

I sent the Sergeant's "explanation" back to the Department of Justice and added my own footnote to the Sergeant's letter which I then sent off to Des Grant, the man who paid out the claims at the Department of Justice: *Des, it may be of interest to note that unfortunately I am a Leitrim man myself.*

Ned's money was paid within a few days, with a little note from Des to me, offering his deepest sympathy on the so and so of a Sergeant I had to deal with.

After almost six months the post office dispute was eventually resolved with the position being given to the niece of the Post Mistress.

***

The months passed by with little else happening and I realised I was becoming bored. Really, there wasn't much to do and all day to do it. On 10 January 1966 I took leave for five days to do a bit of decorating around the house. I was in the midst of wall papering the front room when I had a visitor, Inspector Lee. He came to tell me his good news, 'I've just been promoted to Superintendent!' I congratulated him, 'Where are you going to be stationed?'

'Guess!' I had heard there was a vacancy in Ennis, and knew that his daughter worked as a chemist in Limerick, so I suggested there.

'Nope!'

'Dublin?'

'Nope!'

'Okay, I give up!'

He grinned as he said, 'Castlereagh!' Now, this was a surprise. 'But, what about me?' I asked. There was no way that the station in Castlereagh needed two Superintendents. He shrugged, 'Well, it seems you've been transferred to Drogheda.' I must say it was great news. I was more than ready for a transfer while Nancy was absolutely delighted. For the first time since we married she would be just an hour's drive from her family in Dublin.

With our youngest child, Breeda, just a new-born, it was the ideal time to be settling somewhere that we really believed would be a long term location. As it eventually unfolded, this proved to be the case and Drogheda became our permanent home.

1966: Drogheda

Less than a month after I had finished a complete re-decoration of the house in Castlereagh we moved to Drogheda, renting a bungalow in the seaside resort of Bettystown while we waited for the completion of the building of our house in the town itself. For the first time, we were actually buying our first home! After all my boredom in that quiet district of Roscommon, Drogheda proved to be a rude awakening. For one thing there was a lot more administrative correspondence due to the fact that there was a lot more crime. It was a much busier town, situated as it was on the main artery between Dublin and Belfast.

1966: Why I Disagree With The Death Penalty

One Sunday in November 1966 I was having lunch with my family when I had a phone call from Sergeant Patrick Carr. An elderly man by the name of George Fleming had been found at his home with serious head injuries and had been taken by ambulance to Our Lady Of Lourdes Hospital in Drogheda. His neighbour, Mrs Harrington, was driving her children to eleven o'clock mass when she saw him stagger out of his house, covered in blood, and fall to the ground. Knowing that she could do nothing for him she drove straight to the police station to alert Sergeant Carr who immediately rang for an ambulance and brought three Gardaí with him to Mr Fleming's house.

They had started making house-to-house enquiries before I got there. There were five houses north of the victim's house and three to the south. At one of the houses on the north side they were told of a badly dressed man of about thirty-five years, who spoke with an English accent. He was a "knight of the road" – a beggar – and it seemed, had knocked on all of the doors in the surrounding area, looking for alms.

When I went into Mr Fleming's house I saw that the hall table had been knocked over and there was a metal pot lying in two pieces on the floor. At the same time I remarked that the walls had been recently painted with a vibrant red emulsion.

I knew that the man couldn't have got very far as he was travelling on foot and I immediately called for a search of all the houses on the south side of Mr Fleming's house. It wasn't long into the search when we found him hiding beneath a bale of hay in a shed. He had red emulsion paint on the left sleeve of his coat and a noticeable amount of blood. There was also blood on his hands, his coat and shirt. There were also two grey hairs hanging from a button on the end of one of his coat sleeves. The injured man was grey-haired. All in all, the evidence was damning.

The suspect was physically shaking and seemed distraught at the situation in which he found himself. He admitted to visiting Mr Fleming's house but denied he had been inside it, a denial which was contradicted by the state of his coat. We arrested him and brought him back to the station where we held a conference. Unfortunately Mr Fleming had yet to regain consciousness so he couldn't help us determine if we had the man who attacked him. My colleagues wanted to charge the beggar with causing grievous body harm but I couldn't agree with them. I had done a course in criminology and for various reasons, one of which was no more than my gut instinct, I was not convinced the man we arrested was the attacker. I decided to charge him with vagrancy, to buy myself some time. He was remanded to Mountjoy Jail until the following Friday.

Call it a police instinct but I knew from my experience that when interviewing a suspect it was important to note the small details: the eyes, the facial muscles, the general body language and how they all reacted to a question. When I looked into the Englishman's eyes I could see no guilt whatsoever. There was also the fact that he kept repeating that when he knocked at Mr Fleming's house there was a red racing bicycle resting against the wall outside. No one else remembered seeing this but if there really was a bike then just maybe there was a second person we should be looking for. In any case I had nothing to lose by continuing with my inquiries since we had him in custody. Accordingly I brought him to the local shop and had him point out the type of bike he had seen. We circulated the details of the bike to see if it would yield any new information. A photograph of the bike also appeared on national television courtesy of the RTÉ programme "Garda Patrol" which was broadcast after the nine o'clock news.

That same night, just after ten o'clock, an anonymous phone call came through to the station. Apparently there was a man living in Ballsgrove in Drogheda, who owned such a red racing bicycle. His name was Joe Doyle and he lived with his partner, a former "Lady of the Night". It further transpired he was originally from Belfast. When we contacted the RUC they immediately knew of Mr Doyle as he was wanted for various house-breaking offences. This was beginning to look promising. Having obtained a search warrant I sent two Gardaí out to Ballsgrove, telling them that if they found the bike they were to bring Mr Doyle in for questioning.

Well, they found the racing bike and returned to the station with its owner. I sat down to interview him. At about four o'clock he finally admitted that he had gone to Mr Fleming's house, on the Sunday morning, after first checking that it was empty. He assumed the man was at mass and, therefore, had plenty of time to go through his things. Of course he would not have known that Mr Fleming was a Church of Ireland man and had only left the house temporarily to fetch water from his well. Mr Fleming walked back into his house to find this man rifling through his possessions after finding some thirty-seven pounds in one of the drawers. The intruder grabbed the metal pot from the range and bashed Mr Fleming over the head with it. I was hugely relieved and gratified to learn that my hunch about our first prisoner was correct.

Both men were brought in front of the court in Drogheda the following Friday, before District Justice Dermot Dunleavy. My "Knight of the Road" was up first and I asked the Judge to strike him from the hearing which he did. He was a free man again. I asked the Sergeant to bring him back to the station for a bite to eat and hold on to him until I was free to speak to him, as I was curious to know the whole story. When I spoke to him later, he told me that he knocked on Mr Fleming's front door just as he had done at all the other houses previously. When it was opened by a man covered in blood who then collapsed into him arms, thereby covering his shirt and coat with blood, he panicked and ran off, full sure that if he was found in the vicinity and the man later died he would be blamed for whatever had happened and could end up being accused of murder.

He was very grateful that I had doubted his guilt. I asked him what his immediate plans were and he told me that he only wished to return to London but unfortunately he hadn't a penny to his name. We had a whip around for him in the station and were able to give him twenty-seven pounds. I had a patrol car drop him off at the North Wall from where he got a ferry across the channel.

For years afterwards I received letters from him that were plainly addressed to, "Chief Constable, Drogheda, County Louth". In time he got himself a job and married a nurse. I must admit to having great satisfaction in solving a crime alongside helping someone who was genuinely down on his luck. It's what police work should be all about.

In the meantime Mr Fleming made a full recovery from his injuries about a month after the incident. Mr Doyle was sentenced to twelve months in prison for the attack. The terrifying thing is that if Mr Fleming had died from his injuries and we never heard about the red bicycle, the "Knight of the Road" would, in all likelihood, have been charged with murder based on the evidence we had. In other words, with the death penalty still on the stature books at the time, he could well have been hanged for a crime he did not commit. It doesn't bear thinking about.

The death penalty was only abolished in Irish law in 1990. The last state execution took place in 1954 when Michael Manning was hanged for raping and murdering a nurse.

1969: Murder in Castlebellingham

It was nine o'clock on Saturday, 29 April 1969, when I took a phone call from Sergeant James MacAteer who was stationed at Castlebellingham. He had grim news, the body of a man had been found in Babes Wood, with James adding, 'I don't like what I'm seeing. It looks like he's been shot.' I told James I was on my way, and was in the car minutes later. Given that we knew there were some subversives active in the surrounding area, I assumed it to be an IRA, (Irish Republican Army), shooting.

The man's body was lying on a grass verge beside a ditch. He looked to be in his late twenties. I remember it being a bitterly cold morning; the victim was clothed only in his trousers, underpants and vest. Five two shilling coins lay scattered on the ground, about four feet from the body. His trouser pockets had been turned inside out so it was obvious that whoever had killed him had been searching for something. There was a bad mark on his hip, and a deep wound on his left leg where the trousers were torn and the skin was peeled back. He wore a calliper – a leg brace – on his left leg. Perhaps the most peculiar feature was the fact that someone had removed all the labels from his clothes. It appeared that James was right. There were two neat holes in the back of the man's head, I guessed from two small calibre bullets, though I was surprised not to see any exit wound. He had obviously bled a lot but I could only find one lone drop of blood on a stone that was protruding from the ditch. There were also skid marks in the dirt on the road. In any case, we were definitely dealing with a death in highly suspicious circumstances.

I contacted Headquarters in Dublin, asking for a pathologist to attend the scene. Our own pathologist was on holidays so one was flown in from

Cork to Dublin airport where a patrol car collected him and took him, at speed, to Castlebellingham. When he eventually arrived, along with members of the Technical Bureau, he carried out an initial examination of the body after which he pronounced the man as being a victim of a hit and run. I asked him if he felt the man would have required a walking stick or crutch, gesturing to the leg brace and he agreed that he would have. There was no sign of the stick or crutch in the surrounding area.

To my mind the pathologist had made a peculiar diagnosis and I didn't delay in responding to it, telling him, 'I'm afraid I have to disagree with you. Are you sure it's a hit and run? I've investigated lots of hit and run cases and the culprit usually leaves the scene immediately. Here, the culprit took the time to remove clothing and labels.' I obviously annoyed the pathologist because he gave me a look of pure disgust and disdain and didn't even oblige me with a reply to my question.

Meanwhile, the body was brought to the morgue at Store Street Station in Dublin.

In due course the pathologist filed a second report that appeared to be solidly based on my own opinion that the man was the victim of homicide.

So far we had absolutely nothing to identify the victim. Red paint had been found on another stone which perhaps indicated that a red car was involved. Then, suddenly we had something, from a pub south of Balbriggan where customers described a red car, a Rover, with a Northern Ireland registration. It was a Friday night and the bar was busy enough and several people had noticed the driver of the car and his passenger coming into the bar. The older man walked with crutches, the younger man ordered the drinks, including a treble brandy for his friend. The bar-man told us that in all his years tending a bar he had never been asked for a treble brandy before. One of the regulars got into conversation with the smaller man who said he was a sheep farmer from Australia, on a tour of Ireland and Britain. He had a very strong accent and introduced his friend as a teacher from Birmingham. The regular, a farmer himself, asked the Australian how many pounds of wool he got from a sheep. The answer was astounding, 56lbs. 'They must be f**king elephants!' the regular quipped.

The Northern Ireland registration was a great piece of information. I immediately contacted the RUC and asked them to check for red Rover cars in the car-parks at Belfast Airport. This paid off when I received a phone call from a Detective Inspector who said that they found a Red Rover and when the boot of the car was opened it looked like the inside of a slaughter house, there was so much blood. There were fingerprints on the inside of the boot lid suggesting that the victim had been alive when he was put in there. The car was brought to Drogheda and we moved out in force to start knocking on doors, hoping to turn up something that would help us in the case.

Some days later, a gentleman booked into a hotel in Guernsey for three nights. He paid up front with traveller cheques that had been issued from Barclay's Bank in Birmingham. The name on the cheques was Robert Munro Nish. The hotel receptionist baulked at the state of the cheques, they were dirty and stained with what appeared to be blood. She rang her boyfriend who happened to be a police detective, and he arrived at the hotel to interview the man.

The guest gave his name as Robert Delahunty and he described how, on the previous Saturday, in Birmingham, he met a man who was staying in digs at 35 Robert Road. The banks were closed and he badly needed cash, so he sold three hundred pounds worth of traveller cheques to Delahunty for two hundred and fifty pounds sterling.

The Detective charged him with obtaining money under false pretences. As it happened the man already had a string of previous convictions.

I was told that the British police had no interest in him and that the man had agreed to travel to Ireland for questioning. In other words he knew he was caught. Two Gardaí were sent over to escort him back into the jurisdiction. We gave him a meal at a local hotel and then I interviewed him at the station in Drogheda. He sang like a canary. He told me how he met his victim in Birmingham, a teacher from the United States on sabbatical leave, who sold him two cheques worth three hundred pounds for two hundred and fifty pounds in cash. Delahunty then stayed with Mr Munro Nish at the lodging house on Robert Road. The landlady there, a Mrs

Kilbride from Mayo, was a big help to us in corroborating the information.

We charged Delahunty with murder. The trial was held a few months later in Dublin's Circuit Criminal Court. Delahunty was represented by his senior counsel, Seamus Sorahan, who was one of the best legal brains that this country has ever produced. On the second day of the trial Delahunty made the unexpected decision to sack Mr Sorahan, complaining that he wasn't asking the right questions, and advised that he would be defending himself. In fact it proved to be a wise decision on his part as it transpired that he gave an absolutely brilliant performance in the court room.

The trial lasted five days and finished with a below par summary from the State representative. Delahunty was found guilty of manslaughter – not murder – and was sentenced to four years imprisonment. He was released after three.

Some years later an English TV station wanted to make a documentary about the case, in particular to highlight the cooperation between the RUC, the English police and An Garda Síochána. I was invited to take part in the programme but was advised by my superiors that I would not be permitted to do so. When the documentary aired, one of the narrators made the mistake of saying that Delahunty had been convicted of murder instead of manslaughter as had been the verdict. Delahunty took a civil action against the programme makers and was awarded four thousand pounds.

He described how he accidentally ran over and badly injured Robert Munro Nish when the latter got out of the car to answer a call of nature. Due to the fact that Delahunty had a long string of convictions across the UK he panicked, thinking only to dispose of the body instead of contacting the police. Munro Nish was still breathing when Delahunty put him in the boot of the car. Those two neat holes, that I had taken to be bullet wounds, were actually indentations made by the two prongs on the inside of the boot lid. That was why there was no exit wound. So, this was his defence, that it was an accident. Suffice to say I felt otherwise.

1974 - 1979: Mullingar and Garda Headquarters, Dublin

Having spent eight years as a Superintendent in Drogheda, in 1974, I received news of my promotion to the rank of Chief Superintendent. I was more than pleased to hear that my appointment was to head up the Longford / Westmeath division which meant that I was to be based in Mullingar. With the family well settled in Drogheda, a town which we all had come to consider as 'home' in the long term, I made the decision to leave Nancy and the children where they were while I would take lodgings in Mullingar and make the relatively easy commute back to Drogheda at the weekends and once during the week on a Wednesday evening, if my work schedule permitted.

I found great hosts in the Brouder family in Mullingar. Tommy Brouder, a former chef ran a wonderful bed and breakfast ably assisted by his wife, Kathleen. Returning to a warm welcome and a tasty meal every evening made being away from the family somewhat easier.

Now working at the rank of Chief Superintendent, I felt that the profile of my work had changed greatly from the days when I was more involved with policing at community level. Whilst I always made a point of getting to know and keeping in touch with as many of the locals as I could, the main part of the job was more administrative than anything else. If I said that I didn't miss the 'on the beat', crime solving element of the job, I'd be lying, but at the same time I thoroughly enjoyed making decisions and being in control of such a large area and the number of Garda personnel that involved.

On 7 September 1979 I said a fond farewell to my friends and colleagues in Mullingar when I was transferred to Garda Headquarters in Dublin's Phoenix Park to take up my new role as Personal Assistant to Commissioner Paddy McLoughlin on foot of his request that I be appointed to the position. I had had dealings with Mr McLoughlin on many occasions in the preceding years and I had great time and respect for him, as it transpired, he did for me. I loved this job. The Commissioner was an absolute pleasure to work with. A native of Mallin Head, Donegal, he had proved a brilliant supervisor in his previous role as head of the Garda Technical Bureau, the section which dealt with more serious crimes like murder, assault and fraud.

Mr McLoughlin had great leadership qualities and all who worked with him idolised him. I found, however, that when I went to work for him, he did have one fault and that was his inability to say no to anyone because he was such a gentleman. My role developed into the person who would say no as I was determined to limit the stress for the Commissioner. I continued as Mr McLoughlin's P.A. until he retired in 1983.

My next step was to take up the position as Head of what was known as 'B' branch. Effectively B branch looked after all aspects of Garda personnel, i.e. promotions, transfers, disciplinary issues, all of those elements which in later years evolved into what has come to be known as Human Resources. Unfortunately, when it comes to recalling and re-telling any specific incidents for the purposes of this book, I am very much constrained as it involved great confidentiality, often about matters of some delicacy. Suffice to say, that it was a job I thoroughly enjoyed despite the fact that it carried huge responsibility as I was virtually in charge of the day to day personnel matters for the entire police force.

The only aspect of the job which didn't appeal to me was the daily commute from Drogheda to Dublin, a tiresome journey which of course preceded the opening of the Dublin Belfast motorway which, had it been available to me back then, would have made the drive far easier.

One of the happiest days I have ever spent on the force was the 29th of September 1979, the day Pope John Paul visited Killineer, just two miles outside Drogheda. I was seconded temporarily from my position in Headquarters to join the huge team of Garda personnel who were to direct the security side of the Papal visit. My specific responsibility was traffic control. The sun was high in the sky and thousands of people turned up to catch a glimpse of him, including members of the Church of Ireland. Not surprisingly there was no trouble. The only problem I had to deal with was the shortage of ladies' toilets! At some point during the day I decided it was necessary to commandeer two of the gents' toilets and make them available to the ladies. Sometimes in the job, it was the simplest of actions that often yielded the greatest public satisfaction and this indeed was one of those situations!

1985: Return to Drogheda

When Drogheda's Chief Superintendent Dick Cotterell retired in 1985, I applied to fill his vacancy. Though I was sad to give up a job I thoroughly enjoyed, I was more than ready to give up the commuting to Dublin by then and anxious to live properly with my family again.

Drogheda was a busy division, by this stage, due to its rapidly expanding population but also due to its proximity to the border. In the 1980's, the 'troubles' in the six counties resulted in much criminal activity by paramilitaries and subversives in the Louth / Meath division. As a result, much of my time as commander of the division was occupied by problems related to the Northern situation.

Of all the incidents I ever had to deal with where a fatality was involved, I recall in particular one especially sad occasion during my time in Drogheda. One Saturday night when I was sitting at home watching television with Nancy. Superintendent Brian McCabe rang to inform me that Mary McGlinchey, the wife of Dominic McGlinchey, who was a leading member of the INLA (Irish National Liberation Army), had been shot dead in her home about thirty minutes earlier.

Nancy was well used to my having to leave at a moment's notice. As usual I said to her, 'Expect me when you see me'. I could never tell her when I would be back. That was the trouble with this job, though Nancy never complained about it.

The McGlinchey's house was in Muirhevnamor, Dundalk. Superintendent McCabe told me how Mrs McGlinchey had been bathing her two young boys when the back door was forced open and no less than three masked men came up the stairs and shot her dead in front of her children. They killed her with five bullets, two into her chest, one into her head and two into her side. It seems that she had taken her sons out of the bath and was drying them. When she was hit, the impact sent her back into the bath which was now filled with blood. In fact there was blood everywhere. I don't care what sort of person she was, nobody deserved to die like that and her children certainly didn't deserve to witness such a horrific spectacle, one which I'm sure they have nightmares about to this day.

Following her killing, Superintendent McCabe contacted Mrs McGlinchey's father who arrived in Dundalk Station just after four o'clock on the Sunday morning. A lovely, gentle man, he was understandably absolutely heartbroken over the death of his daughter.

After the post-mortem her body was kept at the Louth County Hospital in Dundalk. A contingent of INLA, (Irish National Liberation Army), members arrived at the hospital. They wanted to bring her body home to Northern Ireland through the town of Dundalk which smacked of a publicity stunt. I refused them permission with the full support of Mrs McGlinchey's father who was adamant that he didn't want his daughter's funeral turned into a paramilitary showcase. Much to the annoyance of the INLA contingent, we brought her body up the bypass and avoided the town altogether as I feared that shots would be fired over the coffin as it passed through the town.

I was much relieved to hand the body over to the RUC who met us at the border. They were remarkably well organised and equipped, something I had always admired about them as a police force. A hearse took the body and it was escorted by ten heavily armoured personnel carriers.

Despite a lengthy and thorough investigation we were unsuccessful in bringing anyone to justice for her murder.

There was another troubling incident when three members of the INLA (The Irish National Liberation Army) were shot in the Rosnaree Hotel, just outside Drogheda on the Dublin Road. Two died at the scene while the third man, who was seriously injured, was rushed by ambulance to the Lourdes Hospital. It was believed that other members of the INLA were responsible for the shootings, following on from an internal feud.

At the hospital I organised armed protection for the injured man as my concern was that whoever it was that killed his companions might well come back to finish off the job. I couldn't take any chances. One of my most trusted Detective Sergeants, Matt Downey, was on duty outside the hospital room where the injured man was being treated, when he was approached by a priest who expressed a wish to speak with the victim. The man was dressed like a priest, looked like a priest and talked like a priest but there was just something about him that did not sit right with my colleague. With a brilliant show of initiative, he recited the prayer, 'Remember man, thou art but dust and unto dust thou shalt return' in Latin and asked the priest to translate what he had just said. When the priest said he was unable to do so, Detective Sergeant Downey searched him and found him to be carrying a gun, obviously intending to kill the injured man. He was arrested and charged with unlawful possession of a firearm.

One of my more pleasant memories which stands out from my time as Chief Superintendent in Drogheda was when the hugely popular American singer, Bruce Springsteen, was coming to perform in Slane on Saturday, 1 June 1985. There had been riots which had marred the entire event the previous year when Bob Dylan had played at the same venue. The day before the concert a spark had been struck and the little village of Slane was subjected to an unruly mob pitching a battle against the outnumbered Gardaí. Three cars were burnt out and countless windows of local businesses, including that of the Garda station, had been smashed. Reinforcements were sent from Dublin and the situation only quietened down at about half past four, on the morning of the concert. Some concert-goers had arrived two days before Bob Dylan took to the stage and had spent most of that time drinking so this was probably a contributing factor.

Bearing all this in mind I was absolutely determined that the Springsteen concert would not be a repeat performance of the previous year. As you can imagine the good people of Slane were more than a little anxious about the upcoming concert and I could well understand why. However I was confident that this year would be different. I had plenty of help from the district Inspectors Pat O'Boyle and Stephen Faughnan, along with Sergeant John Clarke who was in charge of Slane, and between us all, we drew up a crowd control plan for the policing of the concert.

The day of the concert was a beautiful one, the perfect warm and sunny summer's day which in itself set a feel good, positive note to the day's proceedings. A huge crowd turned up from all over Ireland and Britain. At around four o'clock that afternoon, I was sitting in the Garda station in Slane, relieved that so far it had been a peaceful day with no incidents and the crowd seeming good humoured and co-operative and interested only in enjoying the music. I recall saying to Inspector Faughnan, 'Well, we got them in safely so now we just have to get them home safely after the concert is over.' I decided to be proactive in this respect and got out a pen and paper to write the following:

'I wish to pay a warm and well deserved tribute to you all today for your excellent behaviour. You are a credit to your parents, to yourselves, to Ireland and we, An Garda Síochána, are mighty proud to be associated with you.

My thanks also to Bruce Springsteen; he has provided us with a wonderful day's enjoyment.

It is the function of An Garda Síochána to get you home safely but we can only do that with your full co-operation. There could be a rush after the concert finishes and some unfortunate person could get knocked down and trampled which would be the last thing that anyone would want. Please continue your good behaviour and obey the directions from the Gardaí and the stewards.

May God bless you and hopefully you get home safely.

Signed,

Chief Superintendent Michael Bohan

I gave the message to Jim Aitken, the concert promoter and he read it out from the stage, receiving a tremendous applause from the crowd in response. My daughter Gretta was in the crowd with her friends and when she shouted out, 'that's my dad!', she was lifted shoulder high.

The week after the concert Jim hosted a lunch in Slane Hotel for all the senior officers to thank us for our efforts in keeping everyone safe and helping to ensure that the concert had been a resounding success. To my great surprise, he presented me with a Bruce Springsteen golden disc for the excellent policing on the day. It was strongly coveted by Gretta as soon as I got home and even today, it still hangs in pride of place on her living room wall. The local paper ran an article about the event under the title, "Springsteen is the Boss, Michael Bohan is the Chief". In fact I got to meet Mr Springsteen himself on the day of the concert and found him to be a warm and friendly man. I didn't like to confess to him that I wasn't exactly a fan of his music and that in the weeks preceding the concert my children had been spending much time in enlightening me as to the musical legend he was!

1987: Retirement

I retired about a year earlier than I had planned to. As I have said, Drogheda was a busy division with much of my time taken up with the consequences of the unrest in the North. Now I do not want to dwell on this and perhaps am only mentioning the reason behind my early retirement since it was covered extensively by the media at the time.

Suffice to say there was an incident at Ballinaby, in County Louth, with a pursuit involving members of the British Army and persons they believed to have been involved in a mortar attack on Glassdrummond army post which was just over the border in County Armagh. The army had chased the men south of the border and a witness subsequently came forward with the claim that a number of Gardaí had been present at the time.

At a press conference held in Belfast after the event, the Northern Secretary, Tom King, said that the men had been arrested as a result of information supplied by the Gardaí to the British Army. This was patently untrue. I watched it on the news that night and couldn't believe what I was hearing. In my view this statement was potentially dangerous for members of An Garda Síochána, suggesting a relationship between the Gardaí and the British Army that did not exist. Any communication from the Gardaí, regarding northern matters, could only be made with the RUC and vice versa. I made a report to Headquarters and asked that the matter be rectified immediately, through normal diplomatic channels, suggesting that Mr King should withdraw his statement and clarify the matter. I followed this up several times but when it became clear that the matter was not going to be pursued and I received no response to my request, I took the decision to resign from my post in protest.

While I would have wished that my career hadn't ended under the circumstances in which it did, at the same time, I should say that I was more than ready to retire. Nancy was delighted. The job, over the last few years, had involved long hours and a lot of stress. Now I would have time to relax at home with my wife and do more gardening, or whatever else I'd like. I had had a truly wonderful career with the force and if I was a young man again I know that I wouldn't have chosen any other path in life.

There was a huge retirement party held for me at the Boyne Valley Hotel in Drogheda, with a presentation to honour my years of service to An Garda Síochána. It was a terrific night; the party went on until 4am the following morning! An Garda Síochána had given me much more than a job and this point was highlighted when I found myself surrounded by so many friends that night.

Nancy and I enjoyed the next fifteen years together, we did a lot of travelling and caught up with old friends around the country, visiting the various areas I had been stationed at. Then she was diagnosed with cancer in 1999 and died in the Drogheda's Cottage Hospital, in 2002. The whole family was around her when she passed. She had been looked after very well by our local GP Doctor Willie Irwin, our family doctor since we first arrived in Drogheda in 1966 and a good friend to this day. I remember being told by an eminent medical professor that he rated Doctor Irwin as one of the best doctors in the country for the early and correct diagnosis of a complaint.

I must admit that I found the first year very tough. To arrive home in the evening to an empty house was unbearable. She had been my patient audience for nearly fifty years; it was hard to deal with the fact that she was gone. Sometimes I caught myself staring at the vacant chair, the armchair she sat in to watch television. Furniture can take on an almost unimaginable importance after someone dies. For instance there is the kitchen chair she sat in, to have all her meals. It sits at the top of the small dining table, just inside the back door. I have used this chair to sit in, to dictate this book, but I have never sat down on it to eat a meal.

Of course I had to keep going for Michael's sake. I could not give up. Somehow, once I got through the first year, it began to get a little easier, or, if not easier, I began to accept that she was gone. I pray to her and for her every day and look forward to being with her again in Heaven. She was the one who encouraged me to write and I hope she is happy that I have finally realised my lifelong ambition of writing a book.

These days I am at peace with the world and myself. What more could anyone want? Despite my age I am happy. I keep myself busy doing the gardening, visiting old friends and taking as many breaks away as I can. Two retired widower friends and myself love nothing better than taking off for the west of Ireland. Every year I attend the Commissioner's lunch for retired Garda officers at Garda Headquarters in the Phoenix Park, a day I enjoy very much as it's an opportunity to meet up with old friends and tell stories about the old days. I still enjoy a good crime story although due to the problems with my eyesight, I can no longer see the pages, so I now listen to the exploits of Inspectors Wexford and Morse on CD. It is part of my nightly routine, along with the smallest drop of whisky into a glass of lemonade which I thoroughly enjoy. Sometimes, it's life simplest of pleasures which offer the most enjoyment.

My children are a blessing to me: John, Anne, Gretta, Michael and Breeda. They take the most wonderful care of me and I can never thank them enough. Sometimes I feel guilty about the amount of attention I receive, the girls, in particular, never stop worrying about me but I know I am incredibly lucky. A special mention also to my grandchildren, Naoimh, Robert, Emma and great granddaughter Onique.

Michael celebrated his fiftieth birthday this year and what a great night we had with him at his party in the Glenside Hotel in Drogheda.

If I am asked for a wise saying, a motto about how best to live a life, all I can offer is what I always did my utmost to do: Take life as it comes, with its ups and downs, and make the most of it. I hope that is what I have done.

THE END